Does What You Export Matter?

D1526461

Does What You Export Matter?
IN SEARCH OF EMPIRICAL GUIDANCE FOR INDUSTRIAL POLICIES

Daniel Lederman

William F. Maloney

THE WORLD BANK
Washington, D.C.

Contents

FIGURES

TABLES

Acknowledgments

This study was undertaken under the Regional Studies Program of the Office of the Chief Economist for Latin America and the Caribbean. The authors are grateful to the Office of the Chief Economist for Latin America and the Caribbean, the Development Economics Research Group, and the International Trade Department of the World Bank for their support during the preparation of the manuscript. They also gratefully acknowledge funding from the Multi-Donor Trust Fund on Trade executed by the World Bank, International Trade and Integration Unit of the Development Economics Research Group. Augusto de la Torre, Norman Loayza, Otaviano Canuto, Jose Guilherme Reis, Bernard Hoekman, Pravin Krishna, Andrés Rodríguez-Clare, Guido Porto, Irene Brambilla, Ana Paula Cusolito, Francisco Rodríguez, Vittorio Corbo, and Roberto Álvarez, among others, provided insightful comments on our previous work, presentations, and papers that are now part of this manuscript. Shifra Katz, a graduate student at the University of Chicago, provided stellar research assistance for chapter 6 when she was an undergraduate at the University of Maryland. Joana Naritomi, a PhD candidate at Harvard University's Political Economy Group, provided research assistance for chapter 7 when she was a consultant for the World Bank. Finally, the authors acknowledge the invaluable comments from two anonymous referees, Ricardo Hausmann and Cesar Hidalgo. All remaining errors are the authors' responsibility.

Abbreviations

AFR	Africa (Sub-Saharan Africa)
CODELCO	National Copper Corporation of Chile
EAP	East Asia and the Pacific
EMBRAER	Empresa Brasileira de Aeronáutica (Brazilian aerospace conglomerate)
EXPY	Average PRODY of a country's export basket
GDP	gross domestic product
GMM	Generalized Method of Moments
IRCAI	Index of Revealed Comparative Advantage in Innovation
ISI	Import Substitution Industrialization
LAC	Latin America and the Caribbean
MENA	Middle East and North Africa
MERCOSUR	*Mercado Común del Sur* (Common Market of South America)
OECD	Organisation for Economic Co-operation and Development
OPEC	Organization of Petroleum Exporting Countries
PPP	purchasing power parity
PRODY	Average Productivity/Income (Y) of countries exporting a good
RCA	Revealed Comparative Advantage
SITC	Standard International Trade Classification
3SLS	Three-Stage Least Squares

1

Introduction

Does the content of *what* economies export matter for development? And, if it does, can governments improve on the export basket that the market generates through the shaping of industrial policy? This book considers these questions by reviewing relevant literature and taking stock of what is known from conceptual, empirical, and policy viewpoints.

A large literature answers affirmatively to the first question and suggests the characteristics that distinguish desirable exports. Some schools of thought are best known by their colorful metaphors: For example, natural resources are a "curse"; "high-tech" goods promote the "knowledge economy"; a "product space" made up of "trees" (goods) from which "monkeys" (entrepreneurs) can more easily jump to other trees fosters growth. More prosaically, but no less controversially, goods which are intensive in unskilled labor are thought to promote "pro-poor" or "shared growth," whereas those which are skilled-labor intensive are thought to generate positive externalities for society as a whole. Concerns about macroeconomic stability have led to a focus on the overall composition of the export *basket*.

This book revisits many of these arguments conceptually and, wherever possible, imports heuristic approaches into frameworks where, as more familiar arguments, they can be held up to the light, rotated, and their facets examined for brilliance or flaws. Second, the book examines what emerges empirically as a basis for policy design. Specifically, given certain conceptual arguments in favor of public sector intervention, do available data and empirical methods allow for actually doing so with a high degree of confidence? In asking this question, the book assumes that policy makers are competent and seek to raise the welfare of their citizens. This assumption permits sidestepping the debate about whether government failures trump market failures generically: In this sense, the book attempts to "give industrial policy a chance."

Conceptual Issues

Traditional trade theory argues that welfare is maximized when countries specialize in goods that they can produce relatively cheaply. Yet dating from Adam Smith's writings, there have been misgivings about this as the final word which have become the basis for the debates about the the the wisdom of industrial policy. Excellent surveys of the conceptual literature can be found in Pack and Saagi (2006) and Harrison and Rodríguez-Clare (2010), and we do not attempt to replicate them here. The book more modestly aims to lay out basic principles that can help organize and interpret new and existing empirical evidence with a view towards broad policy issues rather than specific programs.

In purely economic terms, there are fundamentally two reasons why producing a good may have benefits not fully captured by the price mechanism, namely Marshallian externalities and rents.

Marshallian externalities offer perhaps the strongest argument as to why market forces may not provide an economy with the optimal basket of goods. These can be defined as local externalities that lead productivity to rise with the size of the industry. These may arise for numerous reasons—such as, local industry level knowledge spillovers, input-output linkages, and labor pooling. However, they are not captured by the market price of a good. Harrison and Rodríguez-Clare show in a simple example that where world prices are taken as given, multiple equilibria exist: The market may dictate that a country specializes in a product without externalities when, with some intervention, it would more efficiently specialize in another good with externalities.

The externality argument is one of the strongest for asserting the superiority of some goods over others. However, two critical caveats highlighted throughout the book merit mention. First, Baldwin (1969) cautions that expanding a sector with potential externalities does not necessarily imply that they will automatically occur if the sector is not organized appropriately. This points to a larger theme to be considered throughout, namely that it may be just as important, or more so, to focus on *how* goods are produced rather than on *what* is being produced. Part II of this book explores the argument that, in fact, it may be altogether inappropriate to take the "good" as the unit of analysis.

Second, in addition to the productivity side of the equation, the price side of the equation should be considered as well. For instance, Rodríguez-Clare (2007) argues that if Mexico can exploit a Marshallian externality in a product, it is likely that the industrialized world and even China can as well and, in fact, probably already have. If this is the case, then the supply of that good has already expanded, and world prices will have fallen to the point where the benefit of the externality has been completely offset. Rodríguez-Clare shows that in this case, the optimal pattern of specialization is determined, in fact, by considerations of a deep, underlying comparative advantage. Specifically, there may be externalities from producing computers in Mexico, but unless Mexico is intrinsically better at producing high-level electronics—due to accumulated know-how, human capital—than the United States, the externality argument is not sufficient for Mexico to prefer them to other possibilities, such as producing Tequila, given that the agave plant is uniquely suited to the climate in Guadalajara.

This argument is mitigated somewhat if there are interindustry externalities, that is, the spillovers accrue to the economy as a whole. The increased productivity in all goods is not reflected in the particular profitability of any one good. In this case, any losses from moving against comparative advantage are potentially offset by the overall gains to the economy. These are the arguments put forth by Tyson (1992) in *Who's Bashing Whom* for defending technology-intensive industries in the United States. Still, governments around the world, seeing the benefits of these goods, could competitively subsidize industries and potentially bid away the economy-wide benefits. However, if the magnitude of the externality is asymmetric between rich and poor countries, developing countries may still reap a benefit from supporting these industries. For instance, the first INTEL manufacturing plant in Costa Rica may teach important economy-wide lessons about the importance of tolerance (precision), the nature of international marketing networks, the best way to spin off new firms from old ones, as well as how to provide timely quality inputs to a global supply chain. Arguably, introducing a new type of microchip-driven product to Silicon Valley would have little additional learning effect there. Hence, the advanced countries should be less likely to subsidize this industry than developing countries, and the global price is unlikely to fall enough to offset all of the potential gains. Further, in practice, trade policies often seem geared toward protecting industries that are having trouble competing (textiles or automobiles in the United States) than toward fomenting industries with likely externalities.

The focus on these price considerations raises the issue of market structure and the desirability of reaping rents when the international product price is higher than the cost of production. Although "rent seeking" carries negative connotations, in principle rents are part of the value-added component, and are desirable from the point of view of a country as a whole. Such rents can arise when industries have increasing returns to scale: Both Boeing and Airbus, if they could dominate the market for airframes, would reap large rents. Increasing returns to scale implies that moving first and fast due to the large sunken costs of production acting as a barrier to entry is potentially more critical than "deep" parameters of comparative advantage. As such, governments may engage in strategic subsidies to guarantee that their champion wins the market.[1] However, rents also emerge in less exotic ways when certain goods offer producers market power.

The barriers to entry posed by natural endowments of mining reserves, for example, generate clear rents to producers and, all other things being equal, make natural resources excellent goods with which to be endowed. Unlike externalities, firms can see these rents and there is no obvious barrier to the market allocating resources efficiently, although there may still be an argument for government intervention aiming to increase an economy's terms of trade in the tradition of the optimal tariff literature.[2]

The discussion of the price effects offsetting Marshallian externalities and of rents highlights the tendency of industrial policy debates to focus excessively on the supply side, thereby ignoring issues of market structure and demand. The price offset highlighted by Rodríguez-Clare is one such case where only the potential production side benefits are considered, with relatively little attention as to how prices may have moved internationally to offset them. More generally, it is extremely difficult for a developing country to enter and survive in a well-established and competitive market dominated by advanced country firms. Nokia's near-death experience entering the saturated television industry in the 1980s is emblematic of such challenges.

However compelling the conceptual arguments in either direction, empirically these effects have proved difficult to document and quantify, let alone permit a ranking of goods by their potential for externalities or rents. Harrison and Rodríguez-Clare (2010) and Pack and Saggi (2006) review much of the literature struggling to document the externalities discussed above, which will not be repeated here.[3] A similar dearth of information exists on the relevant elasticities that might offer insights into market structure and rents. Further, the closest relevant estimates vary across several orders of magnitude.[4] Even where a consistent set of estimated global elasticities are available that might offer some suggestive ranking of goods by characteristics, they do not. Kee, Nicita, and Olarreaga (2008, 2009) estimate *within-country* import demand elasticities for thousands of products at the Harmonized System tariff six-digit level. They find that, on average, goods with the highest price elasticities included cotton yarn (–16.29) and buckwheat (–11.72), but also electronic integrated circuits (–12.89). More generally, Kee, Nicita, and Olarreaga's (2008) estimates suggest that the median price elasticities of differentiated goods are numerically somewhat lower, but not statistically different from referenced-priced goods and homogeneous goods traded in organized exchanges (such as commodities in Rauch's 1999 classification).

It is almost certainly empirical blindness on both counts that has led the most prominent literature arguing the importance of export composition—those defending a natural resource "curse" advocating public support for "high productivity" goods—to have effectively taken the empirical shortcut of identifying goods that are thought to embody desirable (or undesirable) qualities and then testing their impact in aggregate growth regressions. However, such shortcuts may not be reliable roads to the ultimate destination of well-founded industrial policy.

This book is organized into two parts. The first part, composed of chapters 2–4, tackles policy issues related to the quality of trade from the viewpoint of desirable goods or industries. In contrast, the second part, composed of chapters 5–7, tackles the issues through the lenses of within-good heterogenity in quality and production processes, and of a country's overall export or trade structure. Chapter 8 concludes with a brief review of the main policy implications.

What Makes a Good Good?

The three chapters composing Part I explore the *good* as a unit of analysis. Each chapter examines a literature that has argued in favor of certain goods as growth promoting (or inhibiting, as the case may be) and discusses the conceptual arguments and empirical evidence supporting the respective viewpoint.

Chapter 2 on Cursed Goods revisits in some detail the ubiquitous literature on the natural resource curse which has offered numerous arguments over the course of 200 years, for example, the absence of inter-industry spillovers, toxic political economy effects, and so on. Although at both the conceptual and anecdotal levels these arguments are compelling, in the end there is surprisingly little evidence for these particular effects. Indeed, the empirical arguments recur to the aggregate level where it can be argued that the majority of the evidence is, in fact, in favor of a resource blessing. This is emphatically not to deny that in many countries natural resources have been associated with negative consequences and these experiences should be understood and contrasted with the successful growth stories. However, at present the *average* effect of natural resource endowments (and even mining output as a share of GDP or net exports) on growth appears to be positive, although we remain concerned about the challenges posed by export concentration.

Chapter 3 on High Productivity Goods and Monkeys examines recent literature produced by researchers mostly associated with the Kennedy School of Government at Harvard University. This literature argues that exporting products currently produced by rich countries yields spillovers that lead to faster growth. Further, it postulates a learning externality arising from the production of these goods. The evidence in favor of this view relies on cross-country growth regressions to demonstrate the growth-enhancing effects of high-productivity goods. However, these results are relatively fragile, even after exploring some alternative growth-model specifications, which arguably provide a fairer (less strict) test of the underlying theoretical arguments put forth by Hausmann, Hwang, and Rodrik (2007). This may imply that the high-productivity effect may be overstated, or, following our focus on the demand side, it may also be because goods exported by high-income countries, by definition, are already generously supplied by competitive economies and, hence, there is an offsetting low rents effect to any possible productivity externality.

The chapter also revisits the monkey-tree argument of Hidalgo et al. (2007), and suggests that it can be cast as an externality with attendant price offset effects. An irony emerges: Goods that are "close" to other goods in the product space and therefore easy for monkeys (entrepreneurs) to jump to, by definition, enjoy low barriers to entry. Further, the potential for rents from Marshallian externalities is likely to have been dissipated. In addition, historical correlations of indexes of comparative advantage among industries (the underlying workhorse of the empirical product space espoused by these authors) are unlikely to be useful predictors of where the next high-rent, high-productivity goods are to come from. On the other hand, populating a high-density segment of the product space could result in export diversification, which in turn could help reduce macroeconomic volatility, although this dimension was not explored by the original authors.

Chapter 4 on Smart Goods extends the scope for industrial policy by exploring labor market data from 16 Latin American and Caribbean economies. It assesses whether certain types of industries offer human capital externalities. Although concerns about income distribution and pro-poor growth would lead to the conclusion that subsidizing agriculture, for example, could yield growth with higher demand for unskilled labor, it is difficult to think of the market failure (besides capital market imperfections) that would justify such a policy. Specifically, there are many other alternative policies that could redistribute income across the population, such as taxes and transfers. In contrast, it is known from the empirical literature on schooling that the aggregate (social) returns to schooling tend to be higher than the micro-econometric estimates of the returns to schooling for individual workers (Krueger and Lindahl 2001). Consequently, this chapter examines patterns of the "returns to schooling" by looking at whether there is consistent evidence that certain sectors provide higher "skill premiums" or returns to schooling than other sectors. Are there some goods that are "smart" and should be encouraged due to market failures in the accumulation of education?

Following other empirical analyses in this book, this chapter examines whether country effects are more or less important than those related to particular industries, and whether the latter should be looked to to provide the incentives to invest in education. In addition, the chapter assesses the role of exports and export-product differentiation as determinants of industry skill wage premiums. The preponderance of the evidence suggests that country and industry characteristics help explain national differences in the skill premium, but exports in general appear to be an important factor. This could imply that, at most, a combination of orthodox pro-trade policies and rather soft industrial policies in support of exporting activities could be useful in raising the skill premium within countries. This, in turn, could raise private incentives to invest in education and skills that would help national development through the social spillovers of education.

Beyond Goods

The two chapters in the second part of the book raise several issues related to the previous analyses of the good or industry as the units of analysis. It argues that, for a variety of reasons, the assumption of the *good* as a homogeneous unit of analysis, produced in uniform ways across countries, is incorrect in important ways, thus shedding further doubt on the wisdom of pursing product- or industry-centered industrial policies.

Chapter 5 on Export Heterogeneity along the Quality Dimension introduces a newer literature on export quality measured by unit values. It goes to the other extreme by arguing that the important variance across countries is differences of quality *within* narrowly defined product categories, rather than the products themselves. In sum, the issue for development policy is not whether an economy exports wine or microchips; it is about whether the economy produces Chateau Margaux for US$ 2,000 or Charles Shaw's Two-buck Chuck. Without full knowledge of the industry structure, it is difficult to say anything about the welfare implications of specializing in one product over another. However, since average quality rises with level of development, the dynamics of quality (measured by the growth of export unit values) potentially offers insights into the drivers of economic growth by acting as a proxy for the accumulation of underlying factors of production that yield high-quality goods and perhaps greater productivity.

The findings support the argument that certain goods have greater potential for quality growth due to longer "quality ladders" that offer stronger convergence effects toward high unit values. This in itself is a weak argument for industrial policies since there is no obvious market failure that suggests that countries are incorrectly specialized should they find themselves in goods, such as commodities, with shorter ladders. Further, critical factors affecting unit value growth appear to be country specific. In particular, there are factors, perhaps deficient credit markets, poorly articulated national innovation systems, or poor institutions that appear to inhibit growth of unit values even within the same products where advanced country export unit values appear to grow more robustly than those of developing countries.

Chapter 6 on Heterogeneity in the Production of Goods argues that seemingly identical goods appear to be produced with different technologies of production in different countries, thereby implying differing potential for externalities. Looking at historical cases and at patenting activity within disaggregated goods categories, it identifies important heterogeneities. When the Republic of Korea produces computers, it does so in a "high-tech" way that arguably generates knowledge spillovers. In Mexico, this is less the case. The question then becomes whether the discussion should be one of goods or *tasks*. Pushing the underlying themes of the previous sections further, it argues that the global fragmentation of the production process has meant that individual countries contribute tasks to an overall production process, even though their trade statistics may suggest that they are producing an entire good. The emblematic case here is China's "export" of the iPod, of which its labor force employed by a Taiwanese firm contributes just a bit more than 1 percent of value added, just a handful of U.S. dollars. This is not to say that the assembly task it contributes does not offer some inter industry spillovers, but to argue that China produces a "high-tech" good overstates the case. Appearing to develop comparative advantage in such an industry might actually reflect the commodification of stages of the manufacturing process rather than a truly high-tech production activity that is inextricable from skilled labor and innovation. Ideally, it would be preferable to have data on countries' exports of "tasks" as opposed to what stage of the production process crosses their border, but it does not exist. Hence, much of the discussion in Part I, like the bulk of the existing relevant trade literature, might require substantial caveats.

Chapter 7, Trade Quality as Portfolio Diversification, explores whether the nature of the basket of goods, as opposed to its individual goods, matters. Here, concentration in one good effectively provides a negative externality to other industries by inducing excessive terms-of-trade volatility. Thus, the government may have a role in ensuring a more diversified portfolio. In particular, the chapter highlights the role of product innovation for diversification and discusses new evidence of the importance of export diversification for reducing macroeconomic volatility, especially among economies that are net exporters of energy and mining commodities.

Indeed, the evidence seems to suggest that small, poor, and mining-dependent economies tend to have a high concentration of export revenues (at least merchandise exports), which is, in turn, associated with high terms-of-trade volatility. However, net exports of energy and mining are not associated with a higher pass-through of terms-of-trade volatility into growth volatility. Furthermore, agricultural commodity exports appear to be an altogether different case and tend to be weakly associated with export diversification rather than concentration. An important fact for the debate over the merits of industrial policy, highlighted by Easterly, Reshef, and Schwenkenberg (2009), is that across the globe manufacturing exports tend to be highly concentrated and dominated by a few "big hits." Hence, when the overall distribution of export revenues is considered as a policy objective, it becomes clear that traditional notions of industrial policy might be outdated. The slogan "picking winners" becomes more than a challenge for the foresight of central planners with good intentions; it becomes a potentially harmful approach that could increase rather than decrease export concentration.

Chapter 8 concludes with a brief discussion of the main findings and policy implications. The focus is not a comprehensive list of specific programs, and "toolkits" are not provided for designing appropriate industrial policies or examples of international "best practices." Our aim is to draw links between the basic notions of positive externalities, the best available empirical evidence, and the challenges policy makers might face in advocating for different types of industrial policies.

In the end, theory, intuition, and empirical evidence all suggest potentially desirable public policies that go beyond the noninterventionist orthodoxy. For example, findings indicate that there are arguments for supporting efforts at diversification in natural resource exporters and subsidizing exports that raise a country's returns to schooling. More generally, a strong case can be made for "horizontalish" (neutral, on average, across sectors) policies supporting the productivity and quality growth of existing industries and the emergence of the ever-unpredictable new ones, for example, in resolving market failures in the development of trade networks, improvements in quality, investment in research and development, and so on.

However, to conclude, the literature to date offers few reliable empirical guides to the superiority of one type of good over another and hence to the selection of products or industries for special treatment. Further, what emerges consistently is an extraordinary heterogeneity of country experiences *within* product categories. This ranges from identical goods being produced with very different levels of productivity, quality, and technological sophistication, to the fact that, in an evolving global production system, countries increasingly trade in tasks—fragments in the production of a good—rendering the concept of a good increasingly anachronistic. The concern with how countries produce what is currently exported arguably merits more attention than what is produced. Understanding the roots of the observed differential performance, in turn, feeds back into the question of what is exported through conventional considerations of comparative advantage. Throughout this book, simple empirical exercises suggest that country-specific characteristics, rather than goods characteristics, go a long way in explaining the incidence of potentially desirable industrial structures.

With regard to crafting optimal baskets of goods, specific programs and policies that could be part of such a policy stance remain unexplored here. However, this is partly because more analytical work is needed to understand how products within countries' export bundles are correlated in terms of quantities, prices, and factor demands. Without such knowledge, the design of pro-diversification industrial policies must remain the subject of modest policy experimentation with rigorous monitoring and evaluation.

Notes

1. However, even in this case, retaliation can reverse the original corporate profit transfer across the competing economies (or the terms-of-trade improvement in the case when one of the firms is an import-competing domestic monopoly).

2. Even if a country holds market power in the aggregate, a high level of domestic competition could drive the export price to marginal cost and pass along all potential rents to foreign importers. Government imposition of an optimal tariff is effectively an internal coordination mechanism for restricting output of all domestic agents so that the country enjoys the rents itself. The Organization of Petroleum Exporting Countries (OPEC) performs the same service internationally.

3. See also Basu and Fernald (1995) for an example of how difficult it is to econometrically identify spillovers.

4. Goldstein and Khan's (1985) survey estimates price demand elasticities of aggregate exports for several countries, and finds these centered around 1, implying substantial market power across many industries. However, Panagariya, Shah, and Mishra (2001) argue that this contradicts a more mainstream assumption that most countries face very high, even infinite elasticities, for their goods. They find that, at greater levels of disaggregation and with an improved estimation approach, estimates of a set of textile-related products lie between 60 and 136 for Bangladesh. Estimates across a broader range of goods and countries are not available.

Part I

What Makes a Good Good?

2

Cursed Goods: Natural Resources

Perhaps the class of goods that have been considered to have an impact on growth, in this case negative, are those based on natural resources; indeed, a vibrant literature persists on the "resource curse."[1] Adam Smith (1776) was perhaps the first to articulate a concern that mining was a bad use of labor and capital and should be discouraged.[2] The idea reappeared in the mid-1950s in Latin America when Raúl Prebisch (1959), observing slowing regional growth, argued that natural resource industries had fewer possibilities for technological progress. Further, Latin American countries were condemned to decreasing relative prices on their exports. These stylized facts helped to justify the subsequent import substitution industrialization (ISI) experiment in modifying national productive structures. Subsequently, disenchantment with the inefficiencies of protectionism and the consequences of populist macroeconomic policies led to more open trade regimes and less intrusive microeconomic policies, partly with the example of East Asia's rapid export-led growth in mind.

Stylized Facts and the Mechanisms of the Curse

Two stylized facts have emerged to convert a new generation of analysts to believers in the resource curse. First, the liberalizing economies, with some notable exceptions, did not become manufacturing dynamos or major participants in what is loosely called the new "knowledge economy." Further, growth results were not impressive and, in the case of Africa, dramatic falls in commodity prices contributed to negative growth rates. With the increased popularity of cross-country growth regressions in the 1990s, numerous authors offered proof, that, in fact, natural resources appeared to curse countries with slower growth: Auty (1993); Davis (1995); Gylfason, Herbertsson, and Zoega (1999); Neumayer (2004); and Mehlum, Moene, and Torvik (2006), and arguably most influentially, with several authors drawing on their data and approach, Sachs and Warner (1995b, 1997, 2001a, 2001b). Sachs and Warner have argued empirically that since the 1960s the resource-rich developing countries across the world have grown slower than other developing countries. In 2007, Macartan Humphreys, Jeffrey Sachs, and Nobel Prize winner Joseph Stiglitz published *Escaping the Resource Curse,* which adds further credence to its existence. Consequently, the conventional wisdom postulates that natural resources are a drag on development, which goes against the notion that natural riches are riches, nonetheless.

However, there has always been a countervailing current of thought that suggests that common sense is not, in this case, misleading. In fact, numerous authors have challenged the statistical basis of the resource curse. Most recently, evidence supportive of a more positive view was brought together by Lederman and Maloney (2007a) in *Natural Resources, Neither Curse nor Destiny.* Far earlier, notable observers such as Douglass North and Jacob Viner had dissented on the inherent inferiority of, for instance, agriculture relative to manufacturing. Even when Adam Smith was writing the *Wealth of Nations,* the American colonies were declaring their independence on their way to being one of the richest nations in the history of humanity, importantly driven, for a long period, by their endowments of natural resources (see, for example, Findlay and Lundahl, 1994). Other success stories—Australia, Canada, Finland, Sweden—remain, to date, net exporters of natural resources.[3] Latin America's and Africa's disappointing experiences clearly offer a counterbalance to these success stories, but they do not negate them.

Figures 2.1 and 2.2 plot Leamer's measure of natural resource abundance (the log of net exports for net exporters and net imports for net importing countries) over workforce against (the log of) gross domestic product (GDP) per capita. The data show that high levels of income have been achieved by both low and high resource-abundant countries.

The acknowledgment of the important heterogeneity of experiences has led tentatively to a greater circumspection about the impact of natural resources, although not necessarily less enchantment with the term "curse." Humphreys, Sachs, and Stiglitz (2007) begin their book noting that resource-abundant countries *often* perform worse than their resource-poor comparators, and Dunning (2005) speaks of a "conditional resource curse"—that is, under certain conditions, there is a negative growth impact. This is, without a doubt, a more careful way to frame the issue, and it moves the explanation of the heterogeneity of experience to center stage. Yet the notion of a resource "curse" suggests more than the existence of a negative tail in the distribution of impact. It is a statement

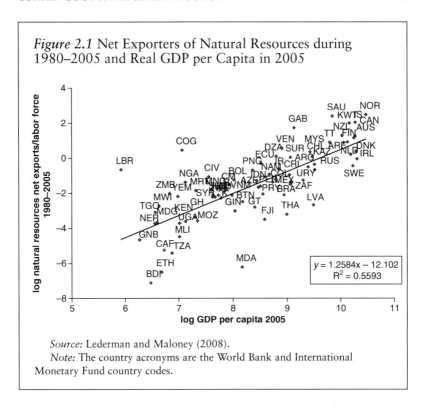

Figure 2.1 Net Exporters of Natural Resources during 1980–2005 and Real GDP per Capita in 2005

Source: Lederman and Maloney (2008).
Note: The country acronyms are the World Bank and International Monetary Fund country codes.

about average impact.[4] Arguably, while colorful, continued use of the term distracts from understanding why some countries have done well with natural resources while others have not.

Numerous channels through which the curse might operate have been offered. First, Prebisch (1959), among others, popularized the idea that terms of trade of natural resource exporters would experience a secular decline over time (meaning without interruption) relative to those of exporters of manufactures. Prebisch is thus perhaps the exception in being preoccupied with the demand side of the quality of export debate, although without identifying any compelling market failure to be addressed. However, even the stylized fact is somewhat in doubt. Cuddington, Ludema, and Jayasuriya (2007) find that they cannot reject that relative commodity prices follow a random walk across the 20th century with a single break in 1929. There is no intrinsic force driving the observed decline, and prices could just as easily rise tomorrow as fall further.

Although commodity by commodity, important mean-reverting components are evident and are, in fact, necessary for stabilization funds to

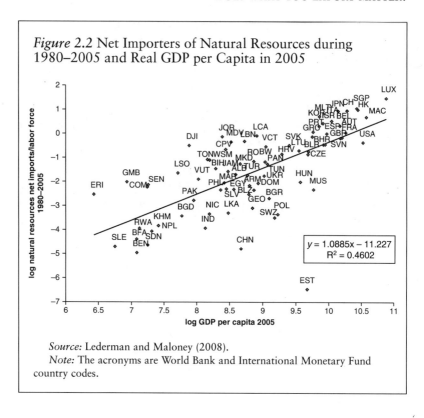

Figure 2.2 Net Importers of Natural Resources during 1980–2005 and Real GDP per Capita in 2005

$$y = 1.0885x - 11.227$$
$$R^2 = 0.4602$$

Source: Lederman and Maloney (2008).

Note: The acronyms are World Bank and International Monetary Fund country codes.

be viable, the notion that long-run prices have a strong unpredictable and permanent component appears more relevant today than at any time during the last half century. Paul Krugman (2008) taking exactly the opposite position from Prebisch, argues that continued growth by China and India, combined with simply "running out of planet," will lead to continued strong excess demand such that "rich countries will face steady pressure on their economies from rising resource prices, making it harder to raise their standard of living."[5]

Second, beginning with Smith, observers have argued that natural resources are associated with lower human and physical capital accumulation, productivity growth, and spillovers. The spillovers argument is closest to the classic externalities argument, but neither is accepted as conclusive in the literature. Even in Prebisch's era, future Nobel Prize winner Douglass North (1955, 252) argued that "the contention that regions must industrialize in order to continue to grow... [is] based on some fundamental misconceptions." Pioneer trade economist Jacob Viner argued, "There are no inherent advantages of manufacturing over agriculture"

(Viner 1952, 72). Consistent with Viner's (1952) early assertion, Martin and Mitra (2001) find total factor productivity growth to be higher in agriculture than in manufacturing in a large sample of advanced and developing countries.

Taking a broader view encompassing interindustry spillovers, Wright and Czelusta (2007) and Irwin (2000) have argued that, contrary to Smith's prejudice, mining is a dynamic and knowledge-intensive industry in many countries and was critical to U.S. development. Arguably, the single most important general purpose technology of the 19th century, the steam engine, arose as a learning spillover from the mining industry. Blomström and Kokko (2007) have argued the same for forestry in Scandinavia where Saab, a car and aircraft producer, and Volvo emerged from truck producers serving the forestry industry. So too, Nokia, the telecom giant, arose from what was originally a forestry company.

The question of why such miracles did not appear in Latin America and the Caribbean points toward Baldwin's argument that such spillovers are not automatic, but depend on how goods are produced. Several authors stress the economic complementarity of essential factors, particularly human capital (see Gylfason 2001 and Bravo-Ortega and de Gregorio, 2007). In a related manner, Maloney (2007) argues that Latin America missed opportunities for rapid resource-based growth due to deficient technological adoption driven by two factors. First, deficient national "learning" or "innovative" capacity, arising from low investment in human capital and scientific infrastructure, led to weak capacity to innovate or even take advantage of technological advances abroad. Second, the period of inward-looking industrialization discouraged innovation and created a sector whose growth depended on artificial monopoly rents rather than the quasi-rents arising from technological adoption. At the same time it undermined natural resource-intensive sectors that had the potential for dynamic growth. Hence, natural resources were produced in a "low-tech" way. The alternate path chosen by the United States, Finland, and Sweden was and is, to an important degree, still open. Røed Larsen (2004) argues that Norway's surge from Scandinavian laggard in the 1960s to regional leader in per capita income was based largely on the opposite strategy to that chosen by Latin America and concludes: "Norwegian Oil is a high technology sector which we may assume has much the same positive spillover effects as manufacturing is supposed to have" (Røed Larsen 2004, 17).

These arguments are central to the discussion surrounding the "Dutch Disease" aspect of the resource curse emphasized by, among others, Gylfason, Herbertsson, and Zoega (1999) and Sachs and Warner (2001a, 2001b), where perhaps through an appreciated exchange rate or classic Rybczinski effects, resource booms depress manufacturing activity.[6] However, if the natural resource sector is not inferior in terms of externalities, then this sectoral shift would be of similar import to the canonical displacement of agriculture by manufacturing.

Third, either for reasons of history or Dutch Disease, countries may develop high levels of export concentration, which may lead to higher export price volatility and hence increased macroeconomic volatility.[7] The externality posed by such concentration is discussed extensively in chapter 6 and appears as perhaps the most important of all. However, it should be noted that this is a more general concern. Dependence on any one export, be it copper in Chile or potentially microchips in Costa Rica, can leave a country vulnerable to sharp declines in terms of trade with attendant channels of influence through volatility.[8]

Fourth, another important literature suggests that natural riches produce institutional weaknesses (see, among others, Auty 2001, 2005; Ross 1999; Gelb 1988; and Easterly and Levine 2002). Tornell and Lane (1999) describe the phenomenon of various social groups attempting to capture the economic rents derived from the exploitation of natural resources as the "voracity effect." Subsequent refinements have focused on how "point source" natural resources—those extracted from a narrow geographic or economic base, such as oil or minerals—and plantation crops have more detrimental effects than those that are diffuse, such as livestock or agricultural production from small family farms (Murshed 2004; Isham et al. 2005). Yet again, this concern is not specific to natural resources, but to any source of rents. Autey, for instance, points to a similar impact of foreign aid. "Natural" monopolies, such as telecommunications, have given rise to precisely the same effects in Mexico. The rent-seeking literature generated by Krueger often focused on the adverse political economy effects arising from trade restrictions. Rajan and Zingales (2003) in *Saving Capitalism from the Capitalists* examine *rentier* mentalities among the corporate financial and manufacturing elite, and the need for developing financial markets that ensure that monopolists and rent-seekers will face a constant threat of competition from new firms.

There is clearly an important agenda in understanding the interaction between political institutions and the emergence of natural resource sectors. Mehlum, Moene, and Torvik (2006) have argued the importance of having strong institutions to minimize rent-seeking activity. Rodríguez and Gomolin (2009) stress the preexisting centralized state and professionalized military as essential to Venezuela's stellar growth performance from 1920 to 1970 after the oil exploitation began in 1920. Dunning (2005) offers a model of how differences in the world structure of resources, the degree of societal opposition to elites, and the prior development of the non-resource private sector help predict the incentives to diversification and political stability. Numerous other contributions could be cited here. Without dwelling on the government failures argument, it is nonetheless worth pointing out that if public governance is significantly worsened by the existence of natural resource rents, then industrial policies which

require an insulated and dispassionate government would seem an undesirable approach to exorcizing the resource curse.

Finally, the Hidalgo et al. (2007) Monkey-Tree metaphor and accompa-
nying neural network estimations suggest that natural resources appear in
the low-density part of the product "forest" relative to other goods, and
might therefore offer fewer possibilities for jumping to other industries.
This perspective will be discussed further in the next chapter, but it is worth
highlighting here that proximity in this sense can be cast as a Marshallian
externality and potentially offers a role for intervention. However, again
keeping an eye on the demand side, although some natural resource sectors might be lonely trees in the product space forest, this also implies that
rents are protected from excessive entry that would drive down a country's
export prices. However, there has been no systematic evaluation of trade-
offs between these two considerations.

The Elusive Resource Curse

Without question, many of the channels discussed may have important
implications for growth, although documenting them individually has
been difficult. However, an important benchmark is whether taking all
these impacts together, resource abundance has, as a central tendency,
curse-like qualities. The literature has used a variety of proxies for resource
abundance, but has not been able to demonstrate this.

By far the best known formal empirical tests for the resource curse
are found in the work of Sachs and Warner (1995a, 1997, 1999, 2001a,
2001b) who employ natural resource exports as a share of GDP in 1970
as their proxy. Using cross-sectional data previously employed by Barro
(1991); Mankiw, Romer, and Weil (1992); and DeLong and Summers
(1992) from the period 1970–1990, there are persistent findings of a
negative correlation with growth between 1970 and 1990, much to
the alarm of many resource-abundant developing countries.[9] Yet this
proxy leads to some counterintuitive results as a measure of resource
abundance. Singapore, for example, due to its substantial re-exports of
refined raw materials, appears to be very resource abundant. Further,
given its high growth rates, it even seems to impart a positive relationship
between resource abundance and growth. Because this gross measure is
clearly not capturing the country's true factor endowments, Sachs and
Warner replaced the values of Singapore and Trinidad and Tobago with
net resource exports as a share of GDP (see data appendix in Sachs and
Warner 1997, 29). While understandable, such considerations extend
beyond these two countries and ideally, a uniform transformation of the
data would be preferred.[10] The issue turns out to be central to the findings of a resource curse. When Lederman and Maloney (2007) replicate

the Sachs and Warner results using either a net measure of resource exports or the gross export measure without the adjustments for the two countries, they find that the negative impact of natural resource abundance on growth disappears.

In fact, even accepting the modified data, the interpretation of the Sachs-Warner results is not entirely clear. Sala-i-Martin, Doppelhofer, and Miller (2004), in their Bayesian search for robust explanatory variables across millions of growth regressions, find a persistent negative sign when the proxy enters. However, it is not robust enough to be considered a core explanatory variable for growth as other variables appear to absorb its influence. In contrast, domestic oil production as a share of national income turns out to be a core explanatory variable and with a positive effect. In a similar vein, Lederman and Maloney (2007) show that, controlling for fixed effects in a panel context, the negative impact of resources also disappears, suggesting that it may not be their particular proxy, but its correlation with unobserved country characteristics that is driving the appearance of a resource curse. Manzano and Rigobon (2007) concur and argue that the cross-sectional result arises from the accumulation of foreign debt during periods when commodity prices were high, especially during the 1970s, that led to a stifling debt overhang when prices fell. These results, and the analogy to other bubbles, are important, not only because they cast further doubt on the resource curse, but especially because the policy implication is that the right levers to deal with the lackluster performance of resource-rich developing countries in recent decades lie in the realm of macroeconomic policy instead of trade or industrial policies.

Bravo-Ortega and de Gregorio (2007), using the same proxy (as well as resource exports over total exports), also find a negative cross-sectional impact, but trace its origin to a Dutch Disease effect working through human capital. Adding an interactive human capital term suggests that as the stock of human capital rises, the marginal effect of the exports of natural resources on income growth rises and becomes positive. This is broadly consistent with Gylfason, Herbertsson, and Zoega's (1999) argument that a national effort in education is especially necessary in resource-rich countries, although without their hypothesis that resource-rich sectors intrinsically require, and hence induce, less education. However, Bravo-Ortega and de Gregorio find that the point at which exports of natural resources begin to contribute positively to growth occurs at around three years of education, a level achieved by all but the poorest countries in the world.

Sachs and Vial (2001) and Sachs and Warner (1995b) confirm a negative and robust relationship using a second, related proxy—the share of natural resources exports in total exports, and this proved somewhat more robust. However, it again does not make Sala-i-Martin, Doppelhofer, and Miller's (2004) core list of robust regressors. Further, when Lederman and Maloney (2007) include a generic measure of concentration, the Herfindahl Index, using export data disaggregated at 4 digits of the Standard International Trade Classification (SITC), the resource curse disappears. The curse is one of concentration, not resources. This finding is consistent with Auty's (2000) concern about a resource drag on growth arising from the limited possibilities of diversification within commodities. However, Lederman and Xu (2007) and the historical experience of the U.S., Canada, Sweden and Finland, argue that diversification into non-resource sectors from a strong resource base is feasible.

Leamer (1984) argues that standard Heckscher-Ohlin trade theory dictates that the appropriate measure is net exports of resources per worker. This measure has been the basis for extensive research on the determinants of trade patterns (for example, Trefler 1995; Antweiler and Trefler 2002; and Estevadeordal and Taylor 2002).[11] This was Lederman and Maloney's (2007) preferred measure because it obviated the Singapore issue by netting out natural resource imports for all countries in the data set.[12] Lederman and Maloney (2008) also show, using a simple two sector model that it has the advantage of being strictly positively correlated with resource endowments, which is not true of the gross exports measures discussed above. The Leamer measure, in cross section and in panel contexts across the Sachs-Warner data sample period, yielded either insignificant or positive results. Using Maddison's (1994) well-known growth data from 1820–1989, Maloney (2007) finds suggestive evidence of a *positive* growth impact of resources from 1820–1950, but then a negative impact thereafter, driven by Latin America's underperformance.

In fact, the results become more favorable when researchers use proxies even closer to direct measures of endowments. Stijns (2005) finds no correlation of fuel and mineral reserves on growth during 1970–1989. This is consistent with earlier work by Davis (1995) that mineral-dependent economies, defined by a high share of minerals in exports and GDP, did well relative to other countries during the 1970s and 1980s. Across several million regressions, Sala-i-Martin et al (2004) find the mining share in GDP to be consistently positive and in the core of explanatory variables.[13] Nunn (2008) finds a positive partial correlation between the per capita production of gold, oil, and diamonds and GDP per capita in an analysis of long-term fundamental determinants of development, with a special focus on the role of the slave trade and its concomitant economic consequences for African economies. Alexeev and Conrad (2009, abstract) actually find "that contrary to the claims made in several recent papers, the effect of a large endowment of oil and other mineral resources on long-term economic growth of countries has been on balance, positive. Moreover, the claims of a negative effect of oil and mineral wealth on the countries' institutions are called into question." The main contribution of Alexeev and Conrad was to highlight the fact that to identify the effect of oil and mineral endowments on growth, we would need to estimate a growth model with data dating back to the years when the natural resources were originally found. Otherwise, research would erroneously conclude that growth rates many decades after the discovery of the resources are low, even though it is rather obvious that territories with mining resources tend to have high levels of GDP per capita, as in Kuwait, for example.

In sum, there is little reliable evidence to date emerging from the cross-country data for a resource curse. To put it mildly, the alleged natural resource curse is difficult to find in international data and the methods and data manipulations used in well-cited studies that seem to find the curse are contentious. Therefore, this particular shortcut to identifying "bad goods" seems unreliable. The potentially negative effects emerge in models that use natural resource gross exports as a share of total merchandise exports. However, even these results appear to support a "conditional" curse. Indeed, the share of natural resource gross exports in total exports is probably best interpreted as a proxy of export concentration, as in Lederman and Maloney (2007). This is not to say that there are not good and bad experiences with natural resources. Estimating growth regressions in a quantile-regressions context, Lederman and Maloney (2008) did find international heterogeneity in the effect of net exports of natural resources per worker on the growth rate of GDP per capita during 1980–2005; richer countries tended to have a more strongly positive coefficient.[14] However, overall, there is no notable curse of natural resources on growth (or even less so on levels of GDP per capita). Nonetheless, we remain concerned about the challenges for development policy posed by export concentration, which is often associated with natural resources. We will return to this issue in chapter 7.

Notes

1. This chapter borrows heavily from Lederman and Maloney (2007 and 2008) and Maloney (2007). See also van der Ploeg (2011) for a recent summary of some aspects of the literature.

2. "Projects of mining, instead of replacing capital employed in them, together with ordinary profits of stock, commonly absorb both capital and stock. They are the projects, therefore, to which of all others a prudent law-giver, who desired to increase the capital of his nation, would least choose to give any extraordinary encouragement . . . ."

3. See Irwin (2000) for the United States; Innis (1933) and Watkins (1963) for Canada; Wright (2001) and Czelusta (2007) for Australia; Blomström and Kokko (2007) and Blomström and Meller (1991) for Scandinavia. Latin America also offers its success stories: Monterrey, Mexico; Medellin, Colombia; and São Paolo, Brazil all grew to become dynamic industrial centers based on mining, and in the latter two cases, coffee. Copper-rich Chile has been the region's model economy since the late 1980s.

4. A "venture capital" curse is not discussed because 19 out of 20 venture capital-financed firms go bankrupt. If the central tendency is that natural resources have a positive effect, then they remain a blessing, albeit a conditional one. There is a need to understand the complementary factors necessary to maximize it. This is

not different than understanding why Taiwan, China, did better with its electronics industry than Mexico, or that Italy did better with its fashion industry than the Republic of Korea did with "Project Milan."

5. Krugman, Paul, "Running Out of Planet to Exploit," *The New York Times,* March 21, 2008.

6. These arguments are fundamentally modifications of the Rybczynski theorem of the Heckscher-Ohlin-Vanek framework in which it can be shown, using a 2x2 Edgeworth Box, that an increased endowment of one good necessarily implies an absolute fall in the production of the good that is not intensive in that particular factor.

7. Sachs and Warner (1995b) argue that the Dutch Disease leads to concentration in resource exports, which they assume to have fewer possibilities for productivity growth. Evidence shows that net exports of energy and mining products per worker are associated with concentration of export revenues, which in turn are linked to terms-of-trade volatility. This material is discussed in chapter 7.

8. During 1998–2007, microchips accounted for over 25 percent of Costa Rica's total merchandise exports. See Lederman, Rodríguez-Clare, and Xu (2011).

9. The other papers by Sachs and Warner (1995b, 1997, 1999, 2001a, 2001b) contain the basic results of 1995b, at times using a slightly longer time span (1965–1990 instead of 1970–1989), and often including additional time-invariant explanatory variables such as dummy variables identifying tropical and landlocked countries, plus some additional social variables.

10. Numerous countries in Asia and Latin America have a large presence of export processing zones that would, using the gross measure, overstate their true abundance in manufacturing-related factors. The variable also shows substantial volatility over time, reflecting terms-of-trade movements. Hence, the average for the period is probably a better measure than the initial period value that was used by Sachs and Warner in several of their papers.

11. Assuming identical preferences, a country will show positive net exports of resource-intensive goods if its share of productivity-adjusted world endowments exceeds its share of world consumption. Usually, the net exports are then measured with respect to the quantity of other factors of production, such as the labor force.

12. It should be noted that the cited references show that the Heckscher-Ohlin model of factor endowments performs relatively well for natural resource net exports, but performs less well for manufactured goods. The current debate in the trade literature revolves around the question of how the Heckscher-Ohlin model might be amended (by considering, for example, technological differences across countries, or economies of scale) to help better predict the observed patterns of net exports across countries. However, there is no debate about the use of net exports as a proxy for revealed comparative advantage in this literature.

13. It is tempting to view the Bayesian approach to testing for robust regressors as the final word, as in Sachs and Warner (2001b), where the authors (mistakenly) argue that the curse is robust based on the 2000 working paper version of Sala-i-Martin et al (2004). As mentioned, Sala-i-Martin, Doppelhofer, and Miller find a positive effect of the fraction of mining in GDP on growth. However, this approach is not well suited for dealing with biased coefficients or robustness of coefficients over time. That is, the results might change with changes in the time period covered by the data, or by including only exogenous explanatory variables. Furthermore, the Bayesian approach does not yield robust results even in the presence of measurement errors in the GDP data, and therefore yield different results when using slightly different versions of the Penn World Tables purchasing-power-adjusted data. See Ciccone and Jarocinski (2010).

14. Lederman and Maloney (2008) use quantile regressions to test for international heterogeneity in the natural resource variable coefficients. They find that in the long run, net exports of natural resources are positively correlated, with no statistically significant international heterogeneity, with the level of GDP per capita. This implies that countries would be poorer if they did not have natural resources. Still, there is no evidence of a curse, even if it is true that the long-term gains from natural resources had already been absorbed prior to 1980. There is heterogeneity in the growth regressions.

3

Rich Country "High Productivity" Goods

A second prominent literature has sought to categorize desirable goods on the basis of technological sophistication or level of productivity, that is, it is preferable to export sophisticated or what are sometimes termed "high-tech" goods. In fact, this argument is effectively the complement to that surrounding natural resources since such goods tend to be associated with manufactures and, more specifically, electronics and information technologies.

To date, perhaps the most cogent statement of this view is offered by Hausmann and Rodrik.[1] They offer a particular information spillover model that arguably corresponds most closely to the interindustry externality case. Producing a high productivity good signals to all potential entrepreneurs the level of productivity that is possible, leading to a higher level of productivity overall. Since the level of productivity of goods is not known a priori, once an entrepreneur has an experiment that pays off and "discovers" a profitable product, others can easily imitate this success, providing an externality. Empirically, Rodrik and Hausmann's conclusion is that producing products that rich countries produce is more conducive to high growth rates.

Operationally, they develop two measures in "What You Export Matters" (Hausmann, Hwang, and Rodrik, 2007) to assess the level of sophistication of a given country's exports.[2] This approach is also followed broadly by Lall, Weiss, and Zhang (2006), although without the subsequent step toward showing a link to growth. PRODY (Productivity/ Income [Y] level) is the trade-weighted income of countries producing a particular good. For example, if poor countries produce bananas, banana PRODY will be low; if rich countries produce cold fusion reactors, the reactor PRODY will be high. Value-weighting the PRODYs of the entire export basket of a particular country gives an EXPY (Export Productivity/Income [Y] level), the overall sophistication of a country's exports.

Hausmann, Hwang, and Rodrik (2007) find EXPY to be correlated with growth.

The approach offers a new type of externality and an innovative way of capturing the corresponding measure of good quality. There are, however, arguably several critiques to this approach. First, conceptually, although the focus on motivating PRODY and EXPY is largely heuristic and not meant to be empirically validated per se, conceptually, it is still subject to the Rodríquez critique and abstracts from issues of rents that are potentially important. A good that is very established within very mature markets is likely to have few rents left and will not be very competitive. A prime example of this occurred in the 1980s when Nokia ventured into producing televisions. To use our present terminology, televisions had a high PRODY, but the market was thoroughly saturated and Nokia nearly went bankrupt as a result. Were it not for a small division producing a product (cell phones) that would not even show up in our present PRODY calculations because it did not yet exist, Finland's largest company would be bankrupt (see Blomström and Kokko 2007).

In this context, if countries really did have reasonable latitude in choosing to produce rich country goods, this also implies that other countries do too. Again, those industries will become extremely competitive. Pack and Saggi (2006), for example, argue that the Asian model of the past is exhausted simply because if, before, advanced technology could be combined with cheap labor, the entry of China and potentially other competitors has driven the rents arising from this combination to nothing. Similarly, if "deep" comparative advantage is not so critical for a multinational company to set up a shop in one country versus another, it also means that a multinational corporation has little to keep it there in the face of small perturbations.

Second, empirically, transportation costs, protection, and other factors affect the composition of the rich country exports. Entrepôts like Singapore are reexporting goods that are independent of their actual production structure; hence, the finding that in 1991 "Asses, mules and hinnies, live" had the highest PRODY value.

Finally, as we will discuss in chapter 6, the fragmentation of the global production process renders assignment of a product to an export increasingly irrelevant. For example, the fact that China exports the iPod may not imply that it is acquiring substantial learning from it.

These considerations may simply be adding "noise" to the PRODY estimates, or they may constitute a systematic bias as well. In the next section we take a look at the empirics themselves.

What Are High PRODY Goods?

What are these high productivity goods? Figure 3.1 presents the PRODY values for relatively aggregated categories. Two findings are important.

Figure 3.1 The Distribution of Exporters' Incomes: PRODY and 1 Standard Deviation

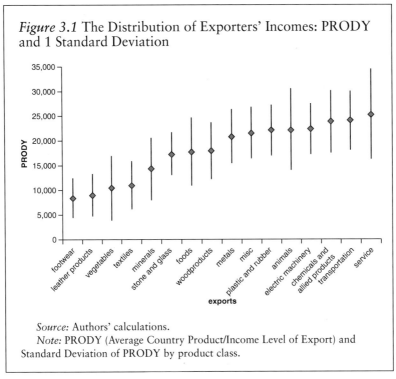

Source: Authors' calculations.

Note: PRODY (Average Country Product/Income Level of Export) and Standard Deviation of PRODY by product class.

First, as perhaps expected, at the high end there is electrical machinery, services, transportation equipment, allied chemicals, plastic, and rubber. At the lower level, there is head- and footwear, leather products, vegetables, textiles, and minerals. In this ranking, the last suggests that natural resources are less desirable. However, second, the highest value is found for service exports, while animals and metals (processed raw ores) are also among the highest PRODY goods. Hence, an intuitive mapping of PRODY to product types is not so clear. Third, there is a high degree of variance in countries producing any particular good, a fact that remains at lower levels of aggregation. This suggests either that a wide variety of countries can, in fact, produce "high productivity goods" and vice versa, or that there is a wide variety of ways of producing a good. Electric machines have high PRODYs, but the nature of the task being produced in the country may be more relevant. This heterogeneity in the level of development of countries producing a seemingly homogeneous product will be revisited in chapters 5 and 6.

Figure 3.2 shows Latin America's EXPYs by country and in international comparison. Although Bermuda, Guadeloupe, Mexico, Brazil, Venezuela, Argentina, and the Bahamas are comparable to, for instance, fast-growing China, overall the Latin America and the Caribbean region is

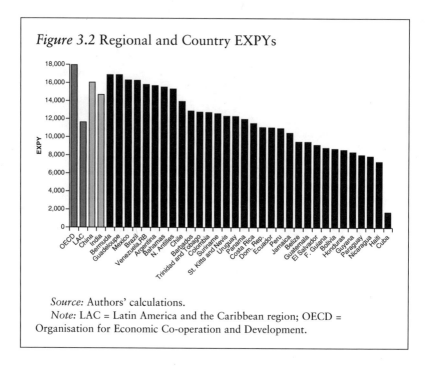

Figure 3.2 Regional and Country EXPYs

Source: Authors' calculations.
Note: LAC = Latin America and the Caribbean region; OECD =
Organisation for Economic Co-operation and Development.

substantially below. Indeed, several large countries—Colombia, Peru, and even Chile—are substantially below these relatively poorer countries. At first glance, then, the idea that this may explain part of Latin America's low growth seems plausible.

As in the case for the resource curse, PRODY, as a shortcut for identifying desirable export baskets, rises or falls on its empirical validation. To date, the literature using PRODY and EXPY is effectively restricted to their inventors, who find a strong relationship between EXPY and growth.

Revisiting these regressions, however, casts some doubt on EXPY's stimulative power and suggests alternative explanations for its appearance. Column 1 in table 3.1 replicates Hausmann, Hwang, and Rodrik's, results, demonstrating that EXPY leads to higher growth. The convergence term (log gdp) is negative and of predicted sign; EXPY is positive and strongly significant for both the Instrumental Variables (IV) and Generalized Method of Moments (GMM) regressions. However, including the investment share of GDP, a standard regressor in growth regressions, knocks out EXPY in the GMM regressions (not shown). Although it cannot be ruled out that producing high PRODY goods leads to more

Table 3.1 Influence of EXPY on Growth: Revisiting the Evidence from Hausmann, Hwang, and Rodrik

	Base: HHR's regressions		Including the export Herfindahl and the investment share		With income average expy		Including the export Herfindahl and the investment share	
	IV	GMM	IV	GMM	IV	GMM	IV	GMM
Log (initial gdp)	-0.038 (4.40)**	-0.02 (2.48)*	0.149 (0.64)	-0.007 (0.78)	-0.0166* 1.66	-0.0177 (0.44)	-0.028 (1.40)	0.124 (1.55)
Log (expy)	0.093 (4.58)**	0.053 (2.45)*	-0.583 (0.71)	-0.029 (1.15)	0.102*** (5.10)	0.0504** (2.52)	0.124 (1.55)	-0.028 (1.40)
Category Log (expy)					-0.0577*** (2.89)	-0.01 (1.00)	-0.04 (1.33)	-0.04 (1.33)
Log (primary schooling)	0.005 (1.77)	0.006 (0.89)	0.021 (0.76)	0.011 (1.84)	0.00394 (0.00)	0.00582 (1.84)	0.00207 (0.00)	0.00207 (0.00)
Log (Investment Share)			0.045 (1.05)	0.023 (1.91)			0.00935 (0.94)	0.00935 (0.94)
Root Herfindal Index			-0.666 (0.81)	-0.058 (2.05)*			0.0615 (1.03)	0.0615 (1.03)
Constant	-0.426 (4.28)**	-0.25 (1.96)	3.756 (0.73)	0.272 (1.64)	-0.186*	-0.199	-0.449 (1.12)	-0.449 (1.12)
Observations	285	285	285	285	285	285	285	285
Number of countries	75	75	75	75	75	75	75	75

Source: Authors' estimations.
Note: EXPY = Average Productivity/Income level (PRODY) of Export basket; GDP = gross domestic product; GMM = Generalized Method of Moments; IV = Instrumental Variable.
Regressions include decade dummies.
Robust t statistics in parenthesis, * significant at 10 percent, ** significant at 5 percent, *** significant at 1 percent.

investment, it is more plausible that countries with high investment rates develop the comparative advantage to produce high PRODY goods.

Adding the Herfindahl Index as a measure of export concentration eliminates the effect of EXPY in both estimations (columns 3 and 4). The finding that export concentration is not good for growth is important, and it is likely that natural resource-exporting countries with low EXPYs are also concentrated. However, the finding suggests that it is the concentration, and not the good per se, that matters. Chapter 7 takes up the issue of diversification more directly.

It is possible that this result arises from misspecification of the estimation. The argument in Hausmann, Hwang, and Rodrik (2007) is in fact more subtle than often distilled. They sensibly do not argue that a country should produce the highest PRODY goods, but rather they should adopt the good showing the highest productivity *within the country's comparative advantage*. For example, it is very likely inefficient for Bolivia to produce at the top of the rich country goods. To bring the specification a bit closer to Hausmann et al.'s model, the second panel includes a variable that captures the average EXPY for countries of the same level of income (decile). The interpretation of log (expy) is now "the level of EXPY relative to those generally found at the country's level of income." EXPY is more significant and positive than before in both specifications. The negative category EXPY in the first column could be seen as analogous to an additional convergence term: the higher the EXPY, the less catch-up is possible and the lower level of growth. However, again, the inclusion of investment and/or the Herfindahl Index eliminates any significance on any EXPY variable.

In the end, it is hard to know whether EXPY's unimportance for growth is a result of the difficulty of demonstrating the existence of the kinds of externalities that are the conceptual core of the argument, that is, that what is produced is what matters, that the offsetting effects of saturated markets should be considered, or that other measurement issues that will be taken up in the next section are of significance. What does seem to be the case is that some circumspection is in order in taking PRODY as a rule of thumb of pro-growth quality for policy purposes.

Of Monkeys and Trees

Hausmann and Klinger (2006, 2007) and Hidalgo et al. (2007), among others, have also been pursuing another type of externality as a justification for ranking goods by desirability, customarily termed the "Monkey and Tree" analogy. In this context, a country's product space is likened to a forest with monkeys climbing trees as a metaphor for productivity growth. To capture the evolution of economies, certain goods allow an easier transition to other goods, and, hence, a continuing dynamic growth process. Monkeys climb up trees but at a certain point would need to jump to other trees (new goods), which they can then climb again.

The imagery is attractive, although the ambiguous relationship to standard economic models makes it somewhat difficult to dissect as an argument. It is not conceptually obvious why jumping from tree to tree is preferred to being in one very tall tree, although, in practice, most countries have graduated through industries. Therefore, it is fair to ask what facilitates jumping into new areas. Again, although the link between diversification and productivity is not tight (see Harrison and Rodríguez-Clare 2010), from a volatility point of view, diversification may matter to growth. However, even here, it is not clear that the answer to having one hugely productive, rent-generating tree (perhaps looking suspiciously like an oil derrick) is to diversify production, rather than to financially smooth and hedge across time.

Whatever the benefits of having other trees in proximity, Harrison and Rodríguez-Clare (2010) have come the closest to approximating a mainstream argument by highlighting the analogy from a tree in close proximity to others where jumps are easy to standard Marshalling externalities with the same caveats discussed earlier. In particular, if a good provides easy jumping in one country, then that must be the case in all countries, and international prices must reflect this. Unless a poor country gets asymmetric benefits from such agglomeration, which is plausible as it fills out its industrial structure, proximity effects may be offset. Further, trees in the dense forest are not only easy to jump from, but they may also be easy to jump *to* since there are so many potential trees of origin. The barriers to entering industries in dense parts of the forest must, by definition, be lower, and competition must be higher and rents few.

Other issues arise when reflecting on the relationship between the externalities surrounding proximity and those being captured by PRODY. For example, is there any guarantee that rich country goods are also those in the thick part of the forest? Expectations that frontier goods produced by rich countries, that is, those with the highest quasi-rents from innovation, would, by definition, be at the edge of the forest with the next obvious place for monkeys to jump yet to be invented.

This raises an issue that is present in the previous arguments but especially germane here. In the case of Scotland in the 19th century, mining led to the invention of the steam engine, a transformative technology. Likewise, Saab and Volvo began as trucking companies for the Swedish forestry industry. Scottish and Swedish monkeys jumped to major new sources of economic dynamism. As Blomström and Kokko (2007) stress, Nokia emerged from a forestry company. However, do these trees remain close to each other today, particularly when, as discussed in chapter 6, production is so globally fragmented? Both forestry and mining used to have transportation industries located very close to them in the forest, and had the quality of "transport industry proximity." Does that mean that Chile is likely to develop its own Volvo? Hausmann and Klinger (2007) find that the product space they estimate in 1975 does almost as good a job at predicting jumps between 1995 and 2000 as a product space estimated in 1995, indicating that it is a relevant analytical structure to study the dynamics in a 20-year horizon. However, it is unlikely that the next Nokia will emerge from a forest company again. In fact, it would seem better for Chile to explore whether the genetic modifications it is undertaking to make its salmon more disease-resistant might lead to a cure for cancer, for example—a relationship that could potentially make the country billions. Such a jump, of course, could not be inferred from past relational patterns any more than the steam engine, the cell phone, Google, or the iPhone could be.

Finally, as discussed in chapter 6, it may not be just the distance among trees, but how good the monkeys are at jumping between them. It may not be the nature of the forest, but the level of the Simian capital that is most relevant. Hausmann and Hildalgo (2009, 2010) have, in fact, recently shifted the discussion toward understanding the underlying capabilities required to produce goods and, presumably, to jump among trees. In the case of EXPY, they have moved away from productivity per se. Hausmann and Hidalgo (2009) use information on the structure of the network connecting countries to the products they export to create estimates of the capabilities required to make products. Hidalgo (2010) shows that, in fact, EXPY can be disaggregated into a component capturing income (productivity) and one capturing estimates of the number of capabilities (as derived from measures of relative comparative advantage). These capabilities can be thought of as very specific factors of production ranging from infrastructure to norms, institutions, and social networks. The sophistication of a product relates to the number of capabilities that the product requires, and the complexity of a country's economy is related to the set of available capabilities (see Hidalgo 2010). Certain measures of capabilities, rather than productivity, are correlated with growth and income. Further, some measures are shown to be robust regarding the inclusion of concentration proxies, although the intuition behind these particular measures is not immediately clear.

These discussions reflect a fascinating application of recent advances in studies of networks and merit further discussion. Several issues, however, remain on the table. First, the link between capabilities, or factors of production more generally, and income and growth is expected. What is not yet clear is the link between what is produced and the accumulation of these capabilities. Hidalgo, for example, argues that "countries become what they make." As an argument in favor of supporting certain goods, this can be seen as a restatement of the externalities argument: Production of certain goods will lead to knowledge spillovers beyond that industry. This is not yet supported by the work in the field, and the automaticity of a country accumulating this capacity, as discussed in chapters 5 and 6, remains in doubt.

Notes

1. See, for instance, "Economic Development as Self-Discovery," Hausmann and Rodrik (2003).

2. See, for instance, "What's So Special about China's Exports?" (Rodrik 2006), "Structural Transformation and Patterns of Comparative Advantage in the Product Space" (Hausmann and Klinger 2006), and "South Africa's Export Predicament" (Hausmann and Klinger, 2006).

4

Smart Goods

Education can provide externalities not captured in the private rate of return to schooling. Hence, often implicit in the discussion of the desirability of high-tech industries is the notion that certain goods will provide a greater incentive to the accumulation of high-level human capital and should therefore be favored.[1]

Using this argument as a point of departure, which goods appear to offer a higher incentive to the accumulation of higher level human capital? Relying on research by Brambilla et al. (2011), it is important to consider whether estimated returns to education across industries suggest that certain sectors provide higher "skill premiums." If so, then perhaps public support to industries that provide higher rates of return to schooling could indirectly provide incentives for the private sector to invest in human capital accumulation.

Analogous to the other empirical analyses discussed here, the econometric analyses focus on industry effects on skill wage premiums across as many Latin American and Caribbean economies as possible. In the same spirit of understanding the heterogeneity of experiences within goods, we examine the effects due to goods and the effects that seem country specific. If country effects dominate over industry effects on skill premiums, then we can conclude that it is country rather than industry characteristics that affect skill premiums. Thus, the private incentives to invest in education by workers and private firms could be addressed with national policies that are sector neutral or horizontal. This chapter will also assess the role of exports and export-product differentiation as determinants of the industry skill wage premium, and whether the evidence could support export-related industrial policies.

It is noteworthy that industry-specific skill premiums exist in economies where intersectoral labor mobility is imperfect, thus driving wedges between the wages of otherwise similar workers across industries. The seminal article on efficiency wages by Krueger and Summers (1988) asserts that this might be the case. In fact, most of the vast literature on trade and wages focuses on interindustry effects of trade policy changes or trade shocks. Indeed, numerous contributions focus on the interindustry differences of wages (after controlling for individual worker characteristics). A good example in this literature is Pavcnik et al. (2004). Brambilla et al. (2011) present a stylized model in which unskilled labor is perfectly mobile across industries, but skilled workers are not—which is sufficient to create significant interindustry differentials in the returns to schooling. Also, there is a macro-labor literature dedicated to estimating worker mobility costs through structural empirical models. Both Lee and Wolpin (2006) and Artuc, Chaudhuri, and McLaren (2010) find extremely large mobility costs for workers in the United States. Such costs would also likely be high in Latin America and the Caribbean region.

It should be emphasized, however, that the estimates of skill premiums can be biased in the sense that they may not capture only the effects of educational attainment on real wages across workers. It is well known that such estimates suffer from at least two types of biases, namely, ability bias (or unobserved human capital) due to talented individuals getting both more education and higher wages, and attenuation bias due to errors in worker self-reported information on wages and schooling.[2] The literature is clear in stating that these biases are important, but it is ambiguous about which one dominates. In the spirit of giving industrial policy a chance, a discussion of some econometric issues in the estimation of the skill premium across industries and countries will be undertaken, without taking a firm stance on these biases. This approach essentially provides a greater scope for industrial policies, as the estimated skill premiums will be assumed not to be due to ability bias.

Further, institutions may play important roles in determining skill premiums. Unions, for instance, may lead to compression of the wage structure, or more generally differential rewards to workers with different skill types. To the degree that some industries are more favorable to unionization than others, this may bias the results. Further, efficiency wage considerations may lead to premiums dependent on the nature of the technology of production of certain types of goods. Indeed, commonalities of premiums across industries have been interpreted as evidence of precisely this kind of effect (for example, Romaguera 1991).

Box 4.1 discusses the basic elements of wage models that are routinely used to estimate wage premiums. Such information is needed to understand where the variable of interest comes from. In turn, this chapter will deal with the relationship between wages and educational outcomes (specifically, the ratio of skilled over unskilled workers), which are the most obvious country-level characteristic that could affect relative wages as it captures the relative supply of skilled workers. The countries covered by Brambilla et al. (2011) include: Argentina, Brazil, Chile, Colombia, Costa Rica, Dominican Republic, Ecuador, El Salvador, Guatemala, Honduras, Mexico, Nicaragua, Panama, Paraguay, Peru, and Uruguay.

Box 4.1 Estimating Skill Wage Premiums

The workhorse of the literature on the returns to schooling or the skill premium is the so-called Mincerian wage equation. It entails econometrically estimating the relationship between real wages and the indicators of educational attainment, while also controlling for other worker characteristics that can affect wages. The model estimated by Brambilla et al. takes the following general form:

$$\log w_{ijt} = f\left(Ed_{ijt}\right) + x'_{ijt}\beta + \delta_j + \delta_t + \varepsilon_{ijt}, \tag{1}$$

where the subscript i denotes individuals, j denotes the industry that the individual is affiliated with, and t denotes years. The hourly wage is given by w. It is computed as the reported weekly wage divided by the number of hours worked per week (in several surveys these answers refer to the total wages received and the number of hours worked during the week prior to the survey).

The variable used to construct the skill premium is education, denoted by Ed. In one approach, skilled workers are those with at least a high school diploma. Thus, the function $f(Ed_{ijt})$ becomes a binary variable (Sk) that is equal to one if the individual has at least a high school diploma. Thus, the wage model is as follows:

$$\log w_{ijt} = \gamma SK_{ijt} + x'_{ijt}\beta + \delta_j + \delta_t + \varepsilon_{ijt}. \tag{2}$$

The coefficient γ measures the skill premium; the percentage difference in wages of skilled workers relative to unskilled workers.

Another specification is:

$$\log w_{ijt} = \alpha YEd_{ijt} + x'_{ijt}\beta + \delta_j + \delta_t + \varepsilon_{ijt}, \tag{3}$$

where YEd are years of education. The coefficient α measures the percentage point increase in wages due to an additional year of education. This model controls for individual characteristics in the vector x, and for industry and year effects in the indicator variables δ. The controls included in x are gender, age and age squared, marital status, whether the individual works full time or part time, a dummy variable for individuals in rural areas, and regional dummy variables. It should be noted that estimates from these equations provide correlations in a cross-section of workers, and therefore the estimates should be interpreted as reduced form coefficients measuring the average difference in wages between actual skilled and unskilled workers. These are not to be taken as predictions for specific individuals should they move into the skilled group.

(continued on next page)

Box 4.1 Estimating Skill Wage Premiums *(continued)*

The analysis discussed below concerns the wages in 16 countries: Argentina, Brazil, Bolivia, Chile, Colombia, Costa Rica, Dominican Republic, Ecuador, El Salvador, Guatemala, Honduras, Mexico, Nicaragua, Panama, Paraguay, Peru, and Uruguay. The total sample, after cleaning of the data, contains over 7 million observations.

Source: Brambilla et al. (2011).

The authors estimate average skill premiums for the national economy as well as for the numerous industries within countries. After summarizing the authors' estimates of sectoral skill premiums for 61 tradable and nontradable sectors in each economy, including 23 manufacturing sectors, the chapter reviews empirical analyses of industry and country effects on industry-specific wage premiums, and provides a preliminary assessment of export-related determinants of the skill premium in manufacturing industries.

Wage Premiums and Educational Endowments in Latin America

Table 4.1 contains the basic descriptive statistics of the education and skill variables. The first two columns show sharp differences in average years of education and in the ratios of skilled to unskilled workers across countries (skilled workers are defined as individuals who hold a high school diploma). Average years of education are comparatively high in Argentina (10.73), Uruguay (9.68), Chile (9.1), Panama (8.97), Colombia (8.55), and Ecuador, the Dominican Republic, and Mexico (above 7.9). These countries also show the highest share of skilled workers, ranging from 27 percent in Mexico to 52 percent in Argentina (in Colombia, by contrast, the share is lower). Years of education are lowest in Nicaragua, Guatemala, and Honduras (5.31, 5.70, and 5.92, respectively), but the share of skilled workers is lowest in Nicaragua and Brazil (9 percent and 15 percent, respectively). In the cases of Argentina and Uruguay, the comparatively high observed levels of education and shares of skilled workers are partly explained by survey design. In these two countries, the household surveys covered only urban households. In the remaining 14 countries, the surveys are representative of the rural population as well as the urban one.

Table 4.1 Education and Skill Endowments in Latin America and the Caribbean

Country	Average years of education	Share of skilled workers[a]			Share of highly skilled workers[b]		
		All	Male	Female	All	Male	Female
	(1)	(2)	(3)	(4)	(5)	(6)	(7)
Argentina	10.73	0.52	0.49	0.54	0.24	0.24	0.24
Brazil	7.37	0.15	0.13	0.17	0.25	0.29	0.22
Chile	9.10	0.40	0.39	0.41	0.24	0.25	0.24
Colombia	8.55	0.20	0.21	0.19	0.55	0.55	0.54
Costa Rica	7.68	0.18	0.18	0.18	0.34	0.35	0.32
Dominican Rep.	8.02	0.30	0.28	0.33	0.34	0.34	0.34
Ecuador	8.06	0.32	0.32	0.32	0.33	0.33	0.32
El Salvador	6.20	0.23	0.24	0.22	0.22	0.21	0.17
Guatemala	5.70	0.19	0.22	0.16	0.27	0.32	0.22
Honduras	5.92	0.19	0.19	0.20	0.30	0.37	0.24
Mexico	7.94	0.27	0.28	0.26	0.41	0.45	0.37
Nicaragua	5.31	0.09	0.09	0.09	0.46	0.49	0.42
Panama	8.97	0.37	0.34	0.40	0.31	0.28	0.34
Paraguay	7.45	0.25	0.25	0.26	0.23	0.23	0.23
Peru	7.98	0.23	0.24	0.21	0.45	0.45	0.46
Uruguay	9.68	0.33	0.30	0.35	0.35	0.32	0.37

Source: Brambilla et al. (2011).

Note: (a) The share of workers with a high school diploma or more over the total number of workers. (b) The share of workers with more than a high school diploma over workers with a high school diploma.

Column 5 in table 4.1 presents the share of workers with more than a high school diploma (individuals with tertiary education, some college experience, college degree, and graduate degrees), over the total of workers with at least a high school diploma. The differences across countries are obvious, demonstrating that the composition of the skilled labor force varies across countries. Countries with high shares of highly skilled workers in the skilled group (41 to 55 percent) are Colombia, Peru, Mexico, and Nicaragua. It is important to note that since Nicaragua is the country with the lowest share of skilled workers (with high school), the relatively few workers with advanced degrees tend to reach a high level of educational attainment. Countries with low shares of highly skilled workers are El Salvador, Paraguay, Argentina, and Chile (19 to 23 percent). The participation of highly skilled workers in the total labor force can be obtained by multiplying column 5 by column 2.

Table 4.2 presents the results for the returns to schooling, as well as for the skill premium for the sample of Latin American and Caribbean countries. The first three columns under the heading "Years of education" show the estimates of the returns to schooling for the baseline estimation, from an estimation that utilizes only data from full-time workers (a sub-sample of all workers), and results from a median regression (which is less sensitive to outliers than Ordinary Least Squares [OLS] estimates). The results under the "Skill premium" heading follow the same pattern, but focus on the relative-wage effects of a high school diploma. Both sets of results come from the online appendix published by Brambilla et al. (2011).

As with the skill endowments, there is a notable heterogeneity across countries in the estimated returns to years of schooling and in the skill premiums. An immediate question that emerges is whether the skill premiums (and the returns to schooling) are correlated with the observed share of skilled workers. The evidence appears in figure 4.1: The correlation is negative, suggesting that countries with a higher supply of skilled workers (relative to unskilled workers) also tend to have lower skill premiums. Hence, country characteristics do matter as determinants of the skill premium. What about industries?

Wage Premiums across Industries

In economies with perfect labor mobility across industries, wages equalize across sectors, and there should be a unique skill premium affecting all skilled workers in the labor market. With departures from that model, including imperfect factor mobility of skilled labor (but also of unskilled labor), wage equalization does not take place, and skill premiums at the industry level can thus result in equilibrium. In the spirit of giving industrial policy a chance, it can be *assumed* that the wages of skilled workers

Table 4.2 Returns to Schooling and Skill Premiums in Latin America and the Caribbean

Country	Years of education			Skill premium		
	Baseline regression	Full-time workers only	Median regression	Baseline regression	Full-time workers only	Median regression
Argentina	0.078	0.079	0.073	0.481	0.474	0.431
Brazil	0.097	0.096	0.087	0.906	0.909	0.908
Chile	0.110	0.112	0.099	0.563	0.567	0.460
Colombia	0.087	0.086	0.077	0.824	0.810	0.727
Costa Rica	0.086	0.086	0.076	0.690	0.677	0.653
Dominican Rep.	0.061	0.063	0.059	0.485	0.489	0.454
Ecuador	0.070	0.071	0.063	0.497	0.493	0.419
El Salvador	0.056	0.057	0.051	0.447	0.442	0.385
Guatemala	0.077	0.074	0.074	0.716	0.661	0.651
Honduras	0.083	0.082	0.080	0.706	0.680	0.644
Mexico	0.086	0.086	0.078	0.642	0.635	0.558
Nicaragua	0.062	0.066	0.056	0.687	0.697	0.655
Panama	0.078	0.079	0.071	0.487	0.482	0.380
Paraguay	0.074	0.072	0.065	0.500	0.464	0.402
Peru	0.057	0.057	0.052	0.401	0.402	0.337
Uruguay	0.088	0.083	0.080	0.540	0.492	0.454

Source: Brambilla et al. (2011, online appendix).

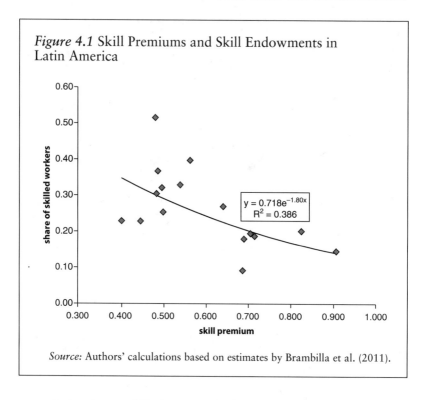

Figure 4.1 Skill Premiums and Skill Endowments in Latin America

$$y = 0.718e^{-1.80x}$$
$$R^2 = 0.386$$

Source: Authors' calculations based on estimates by Brambilla et al. (2011).

across industries can differ because of industry-specific characteristics that make it efficient for employers in some industries to offer higher wages to skilled labor in order to retain them. In short, efficiency wages might be required to retain skilled labor. Furthermore, given the focus on exports, Brambilla, Lederman, and Porto (2012) review the relevant literature and propose a theory that explains why exporting firms will tend to hire relatively more skilled labor and pay higher wages than firms that sell to domestic consumers. In a nutshell, then, the assumption is that selling goods to foreign consumers with higher relative incomes than domestic consumers requires quality upgrading, marketing, and other types of knowledge (for example, knowledge of foreign languages) provided by skilled workers.[3]

To explore this possibility in the Latin America and Caribbean regional data, Brambilla et al. (2011) include interactions between skill categories and industries (defined at the 2-digit level of the International Standard Industrial Classification, ISIC). The results by industry are then ranked within countries (from highest to lowest wage premium). The first column in table 4.3 reports the average skill premium for each sector of employment, ranked from highest to lowest. The list of high-premium sectors, those with an average ranking in the 25th percentile (the top

Table 4.3 Sectors Ranked by Skill Premium in Latin America

	Average	Average rank
Recycling	1.359	4.8
Extraterritorial organizations and bodies	1.237	3.9
Forestry, logging, and related service activities	0.993	16.2
Other business activities	0.941	6.9
Research and development	0.902	14.2
Agriculture, hunting, and related service activities	0.871	15.5
Manufacture of other nonmetallic mineral products	0.851	13.9
Other mining and quarrying	0.836	13.6
Real estate activities	0.819	14.6
Health and social work	0.816	11.5
Manufacture of chemicals and chemical products	0.790	13.3
Education	0.773	14.7
Sewage and refuse disposal, sanitation, and similar activities	0.772	18.5
Wholesale trade and commission trade, except of motor vehicles and motorcycles	0.761	15.8
Mining of metal ores	0.735	22.5
Activities of membership organizations not elsewhere classified	0.721	19.8
Manufacture of coke, refined petroleum products, and nuclear fuel	0.714	19.4
Supporting and auxiliary transport activities; activities of travel agencies	0.703	18.3
Activities auxiliary to financial intermediation	0.692	22.1
Financial intermediation, except insurance and pension funding	0.687	21.1
Construction	0.683	20.9
Electricity, gas, steam, and hot water supply	0.678	20.4
Public administration and defense; compulsory social security	0.653	20.6
Manufacture of paper and paper products	0.628	25.1
Manufacture of office, accounting, and computing machinery	0.626	28.3

(continued on next page)

Table 4.3 Sectors Ranked by Skill Premium in Latin America *(continued)*

	Average	Average rank
Post and telecommunications	0.625	23.3
Manufacture of rubber and plastics products	0.619	26.2
Manufacture of food products and beverages	0.597	24.8
Manufacture of textiles	0.590	23.7
Recreational, cultural, and sporting activities	0.589	25.6
Insurance and pension funding, except compulsory social security	0.571	28.0
Fishing, operation of fish hatcheries and fish farms; service activities incidental to fishing	0.571	25.4
Mining of coal and lignite; extraction of peat	0.568	37.3
Collection, purification, and distribution of water	0.562	29.2
Extraction of crude petroleum and natural gas; service activities incidental to oil and gas extraction excluding surveying	0.554	35.0
Manufacture of tobacco products	0.544	30.1
Manufacture of motor vehicles, trailers, and semitrailers	0.543	34.1
Publishing, printing, and reproduction of recorded media	0.534	30.3
Manufacture of basic metals	0.533	29.7
Air transport	0.528	26.5
Manufacture of electrical machinery and apparatus not elsewhere classified	0.506	34.6
Manufacture of other transport equipment	0.505	32.8
Tanning and dressing of leather; manufacture of luggage, handbags, saddlery, harness, and footwear	0.503	32.9
Manufacture of machinery and equipment not elsewhere classified	0.500	32.9
Retail trade, except of motor vehicles and motorcycles; repair of personal and household goods	0.483	32.8
Sale, maintenance, and repair of motor vehicles and motorcycles; retail sale of automotive fuel	0.483	33.9

(continued on next page)

Table 4.3 Sectors Ranked by Skill Premium in Latin America *(continued)*

	Average	Average rank
Manufacture of radio, television, and communication equipment and apparatus	0.480	29.6
Computer and related activities	0.477	35.4
Water transport	0.475	24.6
Manufacture of wearing apparel; dressing and dyeing of fur	0.467	33.6
Hotels and restaurants	0.442	37.9
Renting of machinery and equipment without operator and of personal and household goods	0.432	35.3
Manufacture of furniture; manufacturing not elsewhere classified	0.414	36.9
Manufacture of wearing apparel; dressing and dyeing of fur	0.414	38.5
Other service activities	0.411	38.0
Manufacture of fabricated metal products, except machinery and equipment	0.397	37.9
Manufacture of medical, precision, and optical instruments, watches, and clocks	0.361	29.4
Land transport; transport via pipelines	0.337	43.8
Private households with employed persons	0.138	47.6

Source: Brambilla et al. (2011).
Note: Dashed lines represent the thresholds for the top and lowest 25th percentiles of industries in terms of their estimated skill premiums.

15 out of 58, listed above the first dashed line in the table) includes numerous nontradable sectors, a few natural-resource intensive industries, and surprisingly few manufacturing industries. Educational services ("Education" and "Research and Development") activities appear in this group, as expected. However, mining activities and agricultural service activities are also at the top of the list. In contrast, manufacture of seemingly "high-tech" goods such as "Manufacture of radio, television, and communication equipment and apparatus" appears at the bottom of the list, among the group of activities in the lowest 25th percentile of the distribution. This list also includes employment in households and leisure and tourism services (such as "Hotels and Restaurants"). Thus, this quick look at the ranking of sectors in terms of their skill premiums

provides at best a mixed picture regarding the desirability of stimulating the growth of industries that are typically considered to be of interest for industrial policies.

Furthermore, as shown in the second column of table 4.3, the rankings of industries in terms of their estimated skill premiums varies notably across countries. This makes it somewhat difficult to precisely ascertain whether a certain industry will be similarly ranked across all industries. This uncertainty by itself should make us cautious about picking industries to be supported by industrial policies in order to raise an economy's average skill premium.

Before proceeding with the analysis of the potential determinants of country-industry skill premiums, the evidence thus far suggests the following:

- There are differences in industry skill premiums, both across countries (for a given industry) and across industries (within countries).
- It is difficult to identify sectors with consistently high (or low) skill premiums across countries. The highest ranking sectors have high average rankings, but the dispersion of rankings across countries suggests that even these sectors rank relatively low in some countries. However, it is abundantly clear that natural resource industries do not systematically pay lower skill premiums. If anything, some appear among the industries with the highest average skill premiums.
- Similarly, the lowest ranking sectors have a ranking of around 35–45. It follows that even these sectors rank relatively well in some cases.
- In the three categories of sectors, high-rank (those above the top dashed line in table 4.3), middle-rank (those in between the two dashed lines), and low-rank (those below the bottom dashed line), tradable or manufacturing sectors are mixed with services and nontradable sectors. There is no clear indication in the data that exportable (or import-competing) sectors do better in terms of the skill premium at the sector level.

Country and Industry Effects on Skill Premiums

To assess the relative importance of country and industry dummy variables on wages, Brambilla et al. (2011) estimate a series of regressions that explain industry-skill premiums with (1) only country dummy variables; (2) industry dummy variables; and (3) country and industry dummy variables. The results appear in table 4.4, which reports the adjusted R-squared for models estimated with data from all sectors, for the manufacturing sectors alone, and for the nontradable and services sectors.

Table 4.4 Explanatory Power of Industry and Country Effects on Latin American and Caribbean Returns to Schooling and Skill Premiums

	Returns to schooling	*Skill premium*
ALL SECTORS	R-squared	R-squared
Only country dummy variables	0.16	0.32
Only industry dummy variables	0.54	0.37
Country and industry dummy variables	0.72	0.66
MANUFACTURING		
Only country dummy variables	0.27	0.51
Only industry dummy variables	0.34	0.19
Country and industry dummy variables	0.55	0.68
NON-TRADABLES AND SERVICES		
Only country dummy variables	0.14	0.27
Only industry dummy variables	0.62	0.48
Country and industry dummy variables	0.80	0.70

Source: Brambilla et al. (2011).

Country dummy variables by themselves account for 16 percent of the variance of the returns to schooling, and about 32 percent of the variance of the skill premiums. Industry dummy variables alone account for almost 54 percent of the returns to schooling and 37 percent of the skill premiums. Both sets of dummy variables explain 72 percent of the variation in the returns to schooling and 66 percent of the variance in the returns to skill premiums. The dummy variables are always jointly statistically significant. In this case, it appears that the industry dummy variables play a more important role than the country dummy variables. It should be kept in mind, however, that the comparison of the adjusted R-squares is an informal way of assessing the role of country and industry characteristics (dummy variables), because it is impossible to ascertain how national characteristics affect industrial structure and vice versa.[4] Finally, although we do not report the relevant test statistics, it is worth noting that both sets of dummy variables are statistically significant.

The results for manufacturing sectors suggest that country dummy variables and industry dummy variables are similarly important in explaining returns to schooling, but country characteristics dominate in explaining returns to skill premiums. In contrast, for nontradable activities, industry dummy variables clearly dominate in explaining both the returns to schooling and the returns to skill premiums. As with the results concerning all industries, both sets of dummy variables are jointly significant in the sample of manufacturing sectors. This preliminary evidence should at least provide food for thought in policy discussions about policies to promote certain manufacturing industries, because in these industries national characteristics seem to be at least as important as industry characteristics. In sum, this exploratory analysis reveals that in Latin America and the Caribbean, industry effects are more relevant than the country effects for the case of nontradables and services, but both country and industry effects are relevant in explaining the skill premium and returns to schooling in manufacturing industries.

Exports and Industry Skill Premiums

In order to study the role of exports in shaping the wages of skilled workers in Latin America, Brambilla et al. (2011) provide two sets of exploratory evidence. One examines the role of industry exports as a share of national GDP by industry; the other studies the role of export unit values (at the 2-digit level) in determining industry wage premiums.

Table 4.5 reports the results concerning the role of the incidence of industry exports in GDP. The correlation between exports and industry returns to schooling and skill premiums is positive, and this correlation coefficient rises after controlling for industry effects (column 2), but its statistical significance disappears with the inclusion of country effects (columns 3 and 4). However, the positive effect of exports on the returns to schooling reappears after controlling for the level of development of each country (proxied by the log of GDP per capita) and national skill endowments (the log of the ratio of skilled—with completed high school—to unskilled workers). The results for the skill premiums are somewhat weaker, but the partial correlation is also positive after including these sets of controls. Moreover, the evidence suggests that richer countries pay higher skill premiums, and, as expected, countries with relatively more workers who completed high school tend to pay lower skill premiums.

Table 4.6 shows the results concerning the role of export prices (unit values) on skill premiums in Latin America. Neither unit values nor the dispersion of unit values explains the industry skill premium. It is possible that this is a result of the noise in the unit values data. Therefore, Brambilla et al. (2011) reported results, reproduced in table 4.6, that measure the variance of unit values in different ways in attempts to reduce the noise due to measurement errors. For instance, in specification C, where the top and bottom 5 percent of the unit values are trimmed, the dispersion in unit values becomes significant in some regressions. This hints that the scope

Table 4.5 Exports, Countries, and Industries as Determinants of Industry-Skill Wage Premiums

A) Return to Schooling

	(1)	(2)	(3)	(4)	(5)	(6)	(7)	(8)	(9)
Log exports/GDP	0.00250*** [0.00091]	0.00342*** [0.00096]	0.00025 [0.00099]	-0.00027 [0.00120]	0.00252*** [0.00093]	0.00309*** [0.00102]	0.00261** [0.00104]	0.00249** [0.00113]	0.00238** [0.00113]
Log GDP per capita					0.01943*** [0.00344]	0.01340*** [0.00512]	0.01439*** [0.00509]	0.02057*** [0.00592]	0.01968*** [0.00601]
Log skilled/ unskilled					-0.01131*** [0.00320]	-0.00923*** [0.00336]	-0.01247*** [0.00363]	-0.00710** [0.00351]	-0.00899** [0.00411]
Enrollment rate						0.00032* [0.00018]	0.00021 [0.00019]	0.00021 [0.00020]	0.00018 [0.00020]
Export constraints						0.00401 [0.00425]	0.00228 [0.00429]	0.00628 [0.00454]	0.00501 [0.00476]
Doing business index							-0.00010** [0.00005]		-0.00005 [0.00005]
Average firm size								-0.09317** [0.03803]	-0.07769* [0.04188]
Country dummies	No	No	Yes	Yes	No	No	No	No	No
Industry dummies	No	Yes	No	Yes	Yes	Yes	Yes	Yes	Yes
Observations	287	287	287	287	287	287	287	261	261
R-squared	0.026	0.419	0.273	0.608	0.485	0.493	0.502	0.506	0.507

(continued on next page)

Table 4.5 Exports, Countries, and Industries as Determinants of Industry-Skill Wage Premiums *(continued)*

	(1)	(2)	(3)	(4)	(5)	(6)	(7)	(8)	(9)
B) Skill Premium									
Log exports/GDP	0.03292*** [0.00798]	0.03330*** [0.00968]	0.02187*** [0.00687]	0.00375 [0.00913]	0.00997 [0.00714]	0.01707** [0.00788]	0.01817** [0.00808]	0.01997** [0.00883]	0.02098** [0.00891]
Log GDP per capita					0.17993*** [0.02762]	0.12134*** [0.03959]	0.11874*** [0.03985]	0.13265*** [0.04683]	0.13921*** [0.04741]
Log skilled/ unskilled					-0.42187*** [0.02687]	-0.41095*** [0.02791]	-0.40506*** [0.02948]	-0.40962*** [0.02947]	-0.39591*** [0.03314]
Enrollment rate						0.00290* [0.00145]	0.00317** [0.00151]	0.00262 [0.00159]	0.00289* [0.00162]
Export constraints						-0.02069 [0.03309]	-0.01805 [0.03340]	-0.01319 [0.03606]	-0.00466 [0.03727]
Doing business index							0.00022 [0.00035]		0.00038 [0.00042]
Average firm size								0.02015 [0.27825]	-0.10155 [0.30904]
Country dummies	No	No	Yes	Yes	No	No	No	No	No
Industry dummies	No	Yes	No	Yes	Yes	Yes	Yes	Yes	Yes
Observations	285	285	285	285	285	285	285	259	259
R-squared	0.057	0.256	0.562	0.722	0.619	0.626	0.626	0.624	0.625

Source: Brambilla et al. (2011, table 5). Standard errors in parentheses. Significance at 1, 5, and 10 percent denoted by ***, **, and *.
Note: GDP= gross domestic product.

Table 4.6 Export-Product Differentiation and Industry-Skill Wage Premiums

	Years of education			Skill premium		
	(1)	(2)	(3)	(4)	(5)	(6)
PANEL A						
Log unit value	0.0006 [0.0009]		-0.0001 [0.001]	0.0037 [0.006]		-0.009 [0.01]
Log var(Unit_value)		0.00031 [0.0003]	0.0003 [0.0007]		0.003 [0.003]	0.006 [0.006]
Log exports/GDP	0.0024** [0.001]	0.0024** [0.001]	0.0024** [0.001]	0.017** [0.008]	0.016* [0.008]	0.016* [0.008]
Observations	287	287	287	285	285	285
R-squared	0.5	0.5	0.5	0.63	0.63	0.63
PANEL B						
Log unit value	-0.0002 [0.002]		-0.0006 [0.003]	0.024 [0.023]		0.021 [0.023]
Log var(Unit_value)		0.0003 [0.0003]	0.0003 [0.0003]		0.0029 [0.0029]	0.0025 [0.0029]
Log exports/GDP	0.0026** [0.001]	0.0024** [0.001]	0.0024** [0.001]	0.017** [0.008]	0.016* [0.008]	0.015* [0.008]
Observations	287	287	287	285	285	285
R-squared	0.5	0.5	0.5	0.628	0.628	0.629

(continued on next page)

Table 4.6 Export-Product Differentiation and Industry-Skill Wage Premiums (continued)

	Years of education			Skill premium		
	(1)	(2)	(3)	(4)	(5)	(6)
PANEL C						
Log unit value	0.0011 [0.0009]		-0.0009 [0.001]	0.005 [0.007]		-0.004 [0.014]
Log var(Unit_value)		0.0007* [0.0004]	0.001 [0.0008]		0.003 [0.003]	0.004 [0.006]
Log exports/GDP	0.0023** [0.001]	0.0022** [0.001]	0.0024** [0.001]	0.017** [0.008]	0.016** [0.008]	0.016** [0.008]
Observations	287	287	287	285	285	285
R-squared	0.5	0.5	0.5	0.63	0.63	0.63

Source: Brambilla et al. (2010, table 6).
Notes: Panel A: dispersion in unit values measured with the variance of unit values across Harmonized System (HS) codes within a country and 2-digit ISIC industry. Panel B: median of the unit values. Panel C: variance of unit values across HS codes, after trimming outliers. Standard errors in parentheses. Significance at 1, 5, and 10 percent denoted by ***, **, and *.
GDP= gross domestic product.

of product differentiation could be related to the skill premium, probably because product differentiation is a skill-intensive activity, as argued by Brambilla, Lederman, and Porto (2012) and Verhoogen (2008).

A key finding from table 4.6 is that in all the models that control for unit values, sectoral exports are still an important factor in explaining the skill premium. Also, the magnitudes of the estimates are similar as those shown in table 4.5. This means that the link between industry exports and industry skill premiums is preserved after controlling for unit values. This result can be interpreted as a robustness check that supports the important role of exports in determining the premium paid to skills in Latin America and the Caribbean. Nonetheless, from a policy viewpoint, it remains unclear whether industry-specific policies should be deployed to raise an economy's skill premiums (or returns to schooling), because raising exports can be done with sector-neutral approaches.

It is possible that the quality of exports measured in terms of unit values can have important consequences for economic development even if they are not robustly associated with skill premiums. The following chapter addresses the quality of trade from this perspective.

Notes

1. See, for example, Krueger and Lindahl (2001) on the theoretical arguments and empirical evidence concerning externalities from education. However, it is plausible that in some countries the private returns to education can be close to the social returns. For skeptical views with applications to the cases of Italy and the United States, see Ciccone, Cingano, and Cipollone (2004) and Ciccone and Peri (2006), respectively.

2. See Griliches (1977), Card (1999), and Krueger and Lindahl (2001) on the econometric issues that plague estimates of the returns to schooling or the skill premium. In their review of the literature as of 2000, Krueger and Lindahl conclude that there is surprisingly little evidence of ability bias in the literature.

3. To be sure, there are likely to be many other plausible explanations for inter-industry wage differentials other than the export-driven efficiency wages argument. For example, unionization and policy distortions might make some sectors pay higher wages to workers with a given skill level. However, if exports are associated with higher wage premiums, it is unlikely to be driven by unionization, as it is well known that export-oriented industries are less unionized than import-competing and public sector industries.

4. In technical terms, to ascertain the extent to which the variance of country or industry characteristics explains the variance of skill premiums, one would need to know how much of the variance of national characteristics is explained by industry characteristics and vice versa. To draw such estimates, one would need to make assumptions about the relative exogeneity of country and industry characteristics.

Part II

Beyond Goods

5

Export Heterogeneity along the Quality Dimension

The previous discussions of the heterogeneity of country experiences with similar goods point to a larger conceptual issue: Is the good the relevant unit of analysis? Even when disaggregated at very fine levels of categorization, goods show such a high degree of differentiation along several dimensions that talking about them as if they were a unique entity is misleading. The next chapters examine several dimensions of this heterogeneity. First, chapter 5 reviews a recent literature that explores the extraordinary heterogeneity of quality found within a good category, measured by price (unit values). Movements along this quality dimension can be seen as "upgrading" arising from investments in innovative capacities (see, for example, Sutton 2001). However, such movements are not intrinsic to the goods. Rather, they reflect decisions of producers as to where along the quality ladder they locate.

Chapter 6 then looks at three other dimensions. First is a productivity dimension broadly conceived as analogous to quality. That is, assuming a highly standardized product, there may be multiple ways of producing it. Second, the "learning" that arises from the production of a good also varies such that producing a computer in one country may lay the foundations for the emergence of new and more sophisticated industries, but also may not. Finally, and crucially for issues of industrial policy, in this era of highly fragmented global production, goods categorizations on the trade account correspond to such a wide variety of subordinate fragments of the global production chain that much of the discussion of goods should really be replaced by a discussion of trade in tasks.

For each theme across both chapters, the case will be made that it may be less "what" is traded than "how" it is produced.

Export Heterogeneity along the Quality Dimension

This chapter continues exploring the heterogeneity found within goods, this time focusing on what has been called export quality. Within the most disaggregated export categories available, there is an extremely high variance of unit values—total export valued divided by quantity. This "price" has been broadly interpreted as a measure of "quality."[1] This wide range of quality within goods is thought to have far-reaching implications for trade theory, and potentially for growth-oriented trade policy as well. The chapter explores some of these issues through this lens. In particular, it allows a revisiting of an analogous question: How much of the quality of a country's export basket is due to what it produces, and how much is due to how it is produced?

Schott (2004) has argued that the extraordinary heterogeneity within goods turns much of international trade theory on its head. He maintains that much of what is confused for intraindustry trade is, in fact, trade in goods of distinct quality. Further, he posits that there is virtually no evidence for conventional considerations of comparative advantage in terms of the types of good produced, and much in terms of quality. This puts him at the other extreme from views advocating the homogeneous "good" at the center of the analysis. Mukerji and Panagariya (2009) have argued that this statement is too strong, noting that the United States does not export two-thirds of the products it imports. This would suggest that there is still a strong role for modeling what types of goods are exported. However, the point remains that there are many ways of production, even for very narrowly defined goods.

From the development point of view that is of the most interest here, Schott (2004) and Hummels and Klenow (2005) show that average unit values of exports increase with the level of GDP per capita. This suggests that export quality and its dynamics offer a potential window on the growth process and its drivers. At one extreme, Hallak and Sivadasan (2007) have argued that improvements in quality represent the accumulation of "caliber," a factor of production distinct from what drives pure productivity growth. In effect, a high productivity country can produce low quality. Sutton (1998), on the other hand, views both quality and productivity as emerging from the undertaking of research and development broadly construed. Unit value dynamics can help explain the accumulation of whatever common factor drives both, or at the very least what is needed to understand the dynamics of accumulating caliber, which is likely to be highly correlated with productivity.

Beyond the question of what drives the level of quality that a country produces, the fact that different goods exhibit very different lengths of their quality ladder raises a concern analogous to that traditionally found in the resource literature. As Hwang (2006) argues, if a force for convergence that developing countries can exploit exists, then countries with small quality ladders presumably are more limited in growth potential. For instance, many developing countries specialize in commodities which almost by definition, are more homogeneous and would therefore have fewer possibilities for convergence effects than more differentiated products. Country growth rates more generally may, again, depend on which goods they produce.

In neither the case of differential potential for productivity growth nor quality growth is there an obvious role for government intervention. There are no spillovers being postulated and, presumably, firms know the technology of production of their industry and make decisions accordingly. However, the exercise below allows a focus on both the heterogeneity found within narrowly defined products and much of the growth in overall quality of a country's basket, as a loose proxy for overall growth, depends on the goods it is producing versus the environment in which they are produced.

How Do Latin America and the Caribbean Compare in Export Unit Values?

Figure 5.1a compares the median level of export unit values across regions for exports to the United States. Since unit values come in their "units"—US$ per bushel, ton, car, bottle, and so on—the quality leaders (90th percentile) are standardized within each product category to generate a measure of "relative quality." Consistent with Schott's finding, the rich countries of the OECD have the highest median relative quality level. The Latin America and the Caribbean region, the Middle East and North Africa region, and the Sub-Saharan Africa region follow. Eastern Europe and Asia, including the rich economies of Asia (EAP [High]: Republic of Korea, Taiwan, China, Singapore, Hong Kong SAR, China) and emerging Asia (EAP [Low]: China, Philippines, Malaysia, and so on) follow. The Latin America and Caribbean–East Asia counterintuitive finding was discovered independently by Schott (2003). Figure 5.1b disaggregates the Latin America and Caribbean region for reference. The peculiarly high values found for relative quality (and PRODY) in the Caribbean are discussed in box 5.1.

At a product level, the graphs in figure 5.1c offer a hyper-disaggregated view of 12 goods at the Harmonized System 10 level, the finest disaggregation available. The categories were selected using a combination of importance in the export basket of the Latin America and Caribbean region, as well as the representativeness of certain types of goods. Turbofan airplanes are not common in the region, but the success of the Brazilian manufacturer, EMBRAER, does have importance as a potential sector that merits benchmarking.

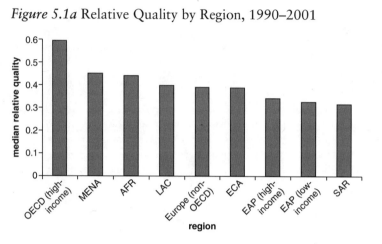

Figure 5.1a Relative Quality by Region, 1990–2001

Sources: Krishna and Maloney (2011) and authors' calculations.

Note: CASIA = Central Asia; EASIAP = East Asia and Pacific; LAC = Latin America and the Caribbean region; MENA = Middle East and North Africa region; OECD = Organisation for Economic Co-operation and Development; SASIA = South Asia; SSA = Sub-Saharan Africa.

The first noteworthy point is that the implicit length of the quality ladder as measured along the vertical axis varies substantially by product. Gold and silver bullion, for example, is concentrated between .8 and 1, with very little vertical differentiation. Footwear, men's shirts, and even microprocessors show values from .1 to substantially over 1. In general, we may expect that commodities, almost by definition, would have less room for vertical differentiation, and this is largely true. Gold, silver, bananas, and fuel oil have relatively short quality ladders. Therefore, Latin America's concentration in commodities may explain its relatively high overall quality. However, this does not extend to all resource-based goods: For instance, the variance in peeled, frozen shrimp and prawns, wine, and coffee is similar to passenger vehicles and aircraft. Overall, though, once the goods produced are controlled for, the region's ranking falls to third-lowest, suggesting that the commodity impact is important.

Even a casual perusal of these figures brings some anomalies to light that point to the difficulty of interpreting unit values. First, the data record imports from countries regardless of whether or not the goods are produced there. Hence, Singapore is a high-quality exporter of coffee (and, as in chapter 3, at times "asses, mules and hinnies") when, in fact, these are reexports through an entrepôt. Likewise, more than one level of

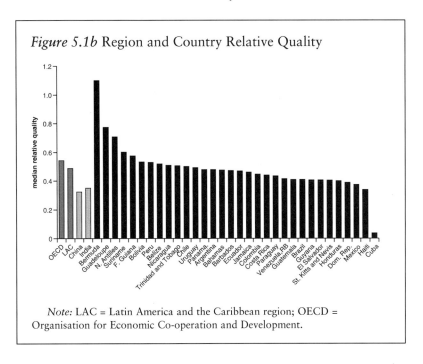

Figure 5.1b Region and Country Relative Quality

Note: LAC = Latin America and the Caribbean region; OECD = Organisation for Economic Co-operation and Development.

the production process may be included. Sweden, in fact, has the highest unit value for coffee (truncated), but this appears to be due to the fact that a particular Swedish company selects and brands the beans it reexports. Second, despite the very high level of disaggregation, there may still be heterogeneity of production along several dimensions other than the most obvious (see Khandelwal 2008 and Hallak and Schott 2008). A high price unaccompanied by substantial sales may be due to other factors that may not actually reflect quality. Third, within a category, countries may export a variety of qualities of wine, exploiting different submarkets, and this may drop the average value far below the "peak" value for country. For example, New Zealand chose to enter the market at a high price point and does not export the cheaper varieties that Chile, Argentina, or, for that matter, France do. Finally, it worth highlighting that it is not clear that being in "high price" goods is obviously better. As Mukerji and Panagariya (2009) note, the United States produces goods at a huge variety of quality levels, suggesting that exporting low-quality goods to certain markets is profitable as well. Acknowledging all of these caveats, the fact that, on average, rich countries produce higher quality goods than poor countries does suggest that, in the aggregate, there is a link.

Box 5.1 Caribbean Super Stars?

In the export quality analysis based on unit values, the extraordinary performance of the Caribbean countries is hard to overlook. In fact, these countries show relative quality, growth in quality, and PRODY levels that are significantly higher than those for China, India, the Latin America and Caribbean region as a whole, and sometimes even the high-income OECD countries. These include such countries as Bermuda, The Bahamas, Barbados, Guadeloupe, the Netherlands Antilles, St. Kitts and Nevis, the Dominican Republic, Trinidad and Tobago, Guyana, French Guiana, and Suriname. Therefore, it is appropriate to examine the trade structures and economic realities that underpin this impressive trade performance.

Some of the Caribbean countries mentioned are top commodities and natural resource exporters. This is the case for Trinidad and Tobago with its petroleum and liquefied natural gas industries, and the Netherlands Antilles with its petroleum shipment and refining industries. Similarly, Guyana and Suriname are important producers of bauxite and gold. French Guiana exports shrimp; Guadeloupe, bananas; and The Bahamas, salt and rum. By focusing on a few, relatively undifferentiated commodities, a country can easily reach a high unit value measurement. Other countries, perhaps due to their geographic position and tax systems, have significantly developed their nonagricultural industries. Bermuda mainly reexports pharmaceuticals; Barbados, electrical components; and St. Kitts and Nevis, light manufactures. These active reexport industries also help to explain the Caribbean outperformance phenomenon.

Still, other causes and questions about the trade performance of the Caribbean countries remain. For instance, the high PRODY levels observed can be due to the homogeneity of the Caribbean trade baskets. As many of these countries have very high GDPs, a given country's PRODY may just be capturing the high income levels of its neighboring export partners. An important question is the relative difference between the aforementioned Caribbean countries vis-à-vis other Latin American island economies such as Haiti and the mainland Central American countries. Ultimately, is it "better" for a country to be a unit value super-performer on the basis of a small set of goods, or to aim at having a relatively more diversified trade basket like Mexico or the Dominican Republic? Finally, the export quality analysis of the Caribbean countries also raises questions about some of the results obtained through this export quality analysis. Although the focus is on broad country, product, and regional trade patterns, it is possible that for some, especially small countries, the data analysis may not be capturing such general trends, but merely some form of entrepôt behavior.

Source: Authors' calculations

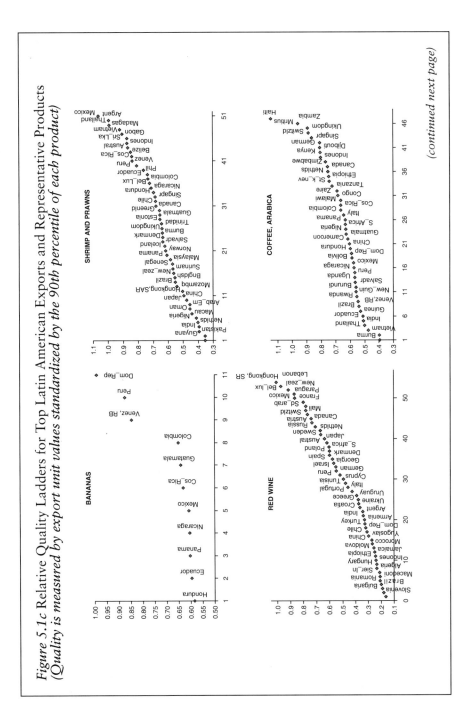

Figure 5.1c Relative Quality Ladders for Top Latin American Exports and Representative Products
(Quality is measured by export unit values standardized by the 90th percentile of each product)

(continued next page)

63

Figure 5.1c Relative Quality Ladders for Top Latin American Exports and Representative Products (*Quality is measured by export unit values standardized by the 90th percentile of each product*) (*continued*)

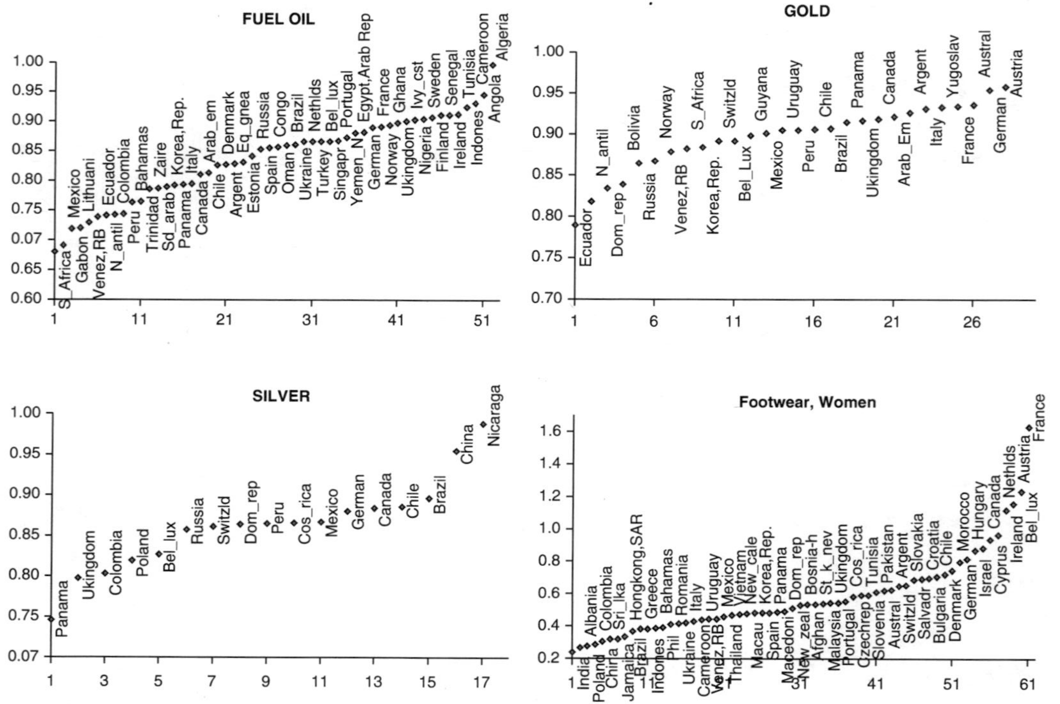

GOLD

Austria
German
Austral
France
Yugoslav
Italy
Argent
Arab_Em
Canada
Ukingdom
Panama
Brazil
Chile
Peru
Uruguay
Mexico
Guyana
Bel_Lux
Switzld
Korea,Rep.
S._Africa
Venez,RB
Norway
Russia
Bolivia
Dom_rep
N._antil
Ecuador

FUEL OIL

Algeria
Angola
Cameroon
Indones
Tunisia
Ireland
Senegal
Finland
Sweden
Nigeria
Ivy-cst
Ghana
Ukingdom
Norway
France
German
Egypt,Arab Rep
Yemen,N
Portugal
Singapr
Bel_lux
Turkey
Nethlds
Ukraine
Brazil
Oman
Congo
Spain
Russia
Estonia
Eq_gnea
Argent
Denmark
Chile
Arab_em
Canada
Panama
Italy
Korea,Rep.
Sd_arab
Zaire
Trinidad
Bahamas
Peru
Colombia
N._antil
Ecuador
Venez,RB
Lithuani
Gabon
Mexico
S._Africa

Footwear, Women

France
Bel_lux
Austria
Ireland
Nethlds
Cyprus
Canada
Israel
Hungary
German
Morocco
Denmark
Bulgaria
Chile
Croatia
Switzld
Slovakia
Salvadr
Argent
Slovenia
Pakistan
Austral
Tunisia
Czechrep
Cos_rica
Portugal
Ukingdom
Malaysia
St._k_nev
Afghan
Bosnia-h
New_zeal
Dom_rep
Macedoni
Panama
Spain
Korea,Rep.
Macau
New_cale
Vietnam
Thailand
Mexico
Uruguay
Venez,RB
Cameroon
Italy
Ukraine
Romania
Phil
Bahamas
Indones
Greece
Brazil
Hongkong,SAR
Jamaica
Sri_lka
China
Colombia
Poland
Albania
India

SILVER

Nicaragua
China
Brazil
Chile
Canada
German
Mexico
Cos_rica
Peru
Dom_rep
Switzld
Russia
Bel_lux
Poland
Colombia
Ukingdom
Panama

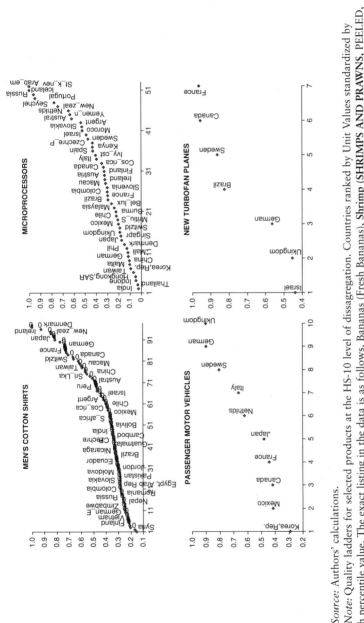

Source: Authors' calculations.

Note: Quality ladders for selected products at the HS-10 level of dissagregation. Countries ranked by Unit Values standardized by 90th percentile value. The exact listing in the data is as follows. Bananas (Fresh Bananas), **Shrimp (SHRIMPS AND PRAWNS, PEELED, FROZEN)**, **Red Wine (RED WINE GRAPE NOV 14% ALCOHOL 2L/LESS OVR $1.05/L)**, Coffee (**COFFEE, ARABICA, NOT ROASTED, NOT DECAFFEINATED)**, Fuel Oil **(FUEL OIL NO 6-TYPE UNDER 25 DEGREES API)** Gold (GOLD BULLION NT UNDR 99.95 P GOLD NONMTRY: GOLD CT), Silver (Silver Bullion, Unwrought), **WOMEN'S FOOTWEAR** (SO R/P UP LTH EXC PGS OT VL OV $2.50/PR WOMEN), Men's Cotton Shirts (Mens' Cotton Shirts, Knit), Microprocessors (**MICROPROCESSORS** MONO IC, DIG, SIL, MOS (ASIC) & (PLA) 32BTS&>), Passenger Motor Vehicles (**PASSENGER MOTOR VEHICLE, NESOI, SPARK IGN, 4 CYL, 1500-3000CC)**, New Turbofan Planes (**NEW TURBOFAN PLANES, NON-MILITARY, >4536 & <=15000 KG)**.

65

These complexities are clearly reflected in Latin America's exports depicted in figures 5.1c, even though the region's overall performance broadly reflects its level of development. For shrimp and prawns, the region (with the exception of Brazil) is in the upper half of the distributions. For wine, it is squarely in the center. Mexico is exporting expensive wines, but these are few and more of boutique interest than mass production along the lines of Italy, which shows substantially lower relative quality. In commodities such as silver and gold, Latin America is predictably close to the frontier.

In footwear, the region is represented across the ladder with Colombia and Jamaica near the bottom, and Chile, El Salvador, and Argentina closer to the top. El Salvador raises the same issue about the degree to which *maquila* (manufacturing operations in a free trade zone) exports of advanced country firms can be considered a product of local "caliber," as opposed to simply the assembly of high-quality products designed elsewhere. The case of men's shirts is similar. Again, Colombia is near the bottom and Mexico, Chile, Argentina, and Peru are in the middle.

Costa Rica and Argentina are in the upper half for a specific type of microchip, again, very likely representing the influence of multinational corporations. Mexico is closer to the bottom. A similar issue is found in passenger cars. Mexico is above the Republic of Korea, but below the other world producers. It is not clear what this means. Mexico exports Volkswagen Jettas to the United States while Germany produces the higher end Volkswagens in Germany. To the degree that these are the same company, clearly, the implicit "caliber" is the same and attributable to Germany, and less to Mexico. EMBRAER is squarely in the middle of unit values for nonmilitary turbofan airplanes, although clearly substantial differences in characteristics may make comparisons problematic.

Unit Value Dynamics

For this study, Krishna and Maloney (2011) examine the dynamics of export unit values, that is, the process of change in quality. This is useful for three reasons. First, their work can be seen as the dynamic analogue to Hummels and Klenow (2005) and Schott (2004). It is known that the unit values of exports of rich countries are higher than those from developing economies, but what are the forces driving this pattern? Second, the analysis of the dynamics of export unit values permits examining whether some products offer better prospects for development via improvements in unit values. Third, one can identify what fraction of aggregate unit value growth is due to goods composition, and what fraction to country-specific characteristics.

Figure 5.2a shows the rate of growth of unit values and figure 5.2b disaggregates these values by countries within Latin America. The OECD shows the highest rate of quality growth, something that, given the higher level of relative quality, indicates that quality is *diverging* over time. However, seemingly paradoxically, there is evidence of convergence *within products*. That is, the export unit values of countries further from the quality frontier grow faster than those closer to the frontier (the highest observed unit value). Thus, the differential position of Latin America and the Middle East and North Africa regions, relative to the high-income economies of East Asia (Hong Kong SAR, China; Taiwan, China, Korea, and Singapore) might explain why they grow more slowly as Hwang suggests. To the degree that these regions are near the frontier in their basket of largely, natural resource–driven goods, they get much less of a catch-up convergence "kick."

However, two other factors of importance emerge from the regression analysis. First, controlling for products preserves divergence but greatly reduces the gap in growth rates between the OECD and other regions. This suggests that what goods countries produce do matter to unit value growth. Second, controlling for the basket of goods, there is a large positive, free-standing OECD effect unrelated to position along the quality ladder. In effect, even if the OECD and developing countries produced the same goods, the countries of the OECD would grow substantially faster, even given their closer proximity to the frontier. This is clear from

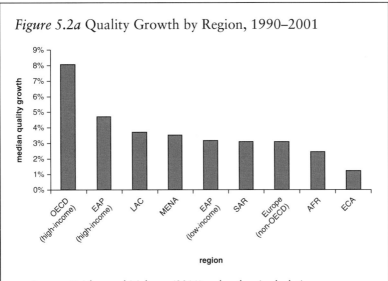

Figure 5.2a Quality Growth by Region, 1990–2001

Sources: Krishna and Maloney (2011) and authors' calculations.
Note: AFR = Africa region; EAP = East Asia and Pacific region; ECA = Europe and Central Asia; LAC = Latin America and the Caribbean region; MENA = Middle East and North Africa region; OECD = Organisation for Economic Co-operation and Development; SAR = South Asia.

Figure 5.2b Region and Country Quality Growth

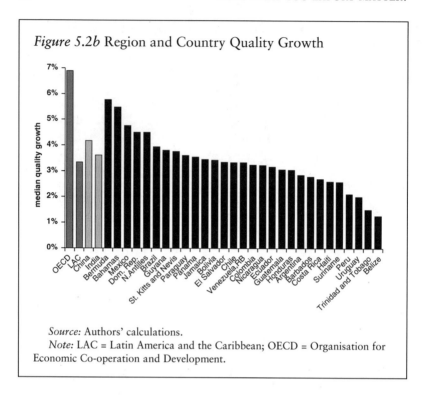

Source: Authors' calculations.
Note: LAC = Latin America and the Caribbean; OECD = Organisation for Economic Co-operation and Development.

figure 5.3, which controls for product composition. The only coefficient that is above average (zero) is that of the high-income OECD countries. Aside from the Latin America and Caribbean region, the coefficients for the remaining regions are lower than zero, indicating that, on average, their growth rate is below average. Clearly, the large fall in the gap between OECD and lesser developed countries' growth rates suggests that the composition of the basket matters to overall growth rates. However, the fact that there is still a divergence after controlling for them suggests that country characteristics remain very important, confirming again that how each good is produced matters greatly.

What Affects the Growth of Unit Values? Countries versus Industries

What factors could influence the rate of growth in unit values? Consistent with findings from the productivity literature, exposure to international competition appears to stimulate quality upgrading manifested in rising

Figure 5.3 Quality Growth by Region, 1990–2001, Product Fixed Effects Included

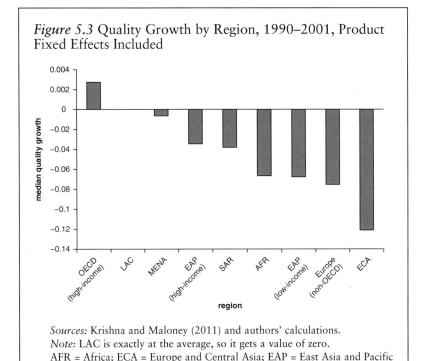

Sources: Krishna and Maloney (2011) and authors' calculations.
Note: LAC is exactly at the average, so it gets a value of zero.
AFR = Africa; ECA = Europe and Central Asia; EAP = East Asia and Pacific region; LAC = Latin America and the Caribbean region; MENA = Middle East and North Africa region; OECD = Organisation for Economic Co-operation and Development; SAR = South Asia region.

unit values. Fernandes and Paunov (2009), using Chilean data, confirm that firms more exposed to trade have higher product quality. The export demand effects are similar. Iacovone and Javorcik (2008) find that Mexican plants invest in product quality upgrading before they export.[2]

The destination market also seems to influence the level of quality. For the United States, in the aggregate, Waugh (2008) found that export unit values rise with the income level of the destination market, and Bastos and Silva (2008) find the same for Portuguese exports.[3] These findings are consistent with different qualities being targeted to distinct submarkets. As Waugh argues, higher levels of quality allow access to more submarkets. Overall, the traditional prescriptions of increasing competition and opportunities to export, especially to wealthier markets, would work in favor of raising quality.

Krishna and Maloney (2010) attempt to unpack the puzzle of the previous section: Although within products there is convergence across countries, without product-specific effects, there is unit value divergence. In other words, countries with higher levels of relative quality appeared to raise their quality faster than those with lower levels. This resonates with the very weak findings of convergence in the growth literature more generally, and recalls the debate as to the reasons this should be the case. It has been suggested, for instance, that poor countries with low levels of physical and human capital may also lack the incentives for rapid accumulation of these factors, thus perpetuating their low income levels. In turn, low rates of return to accumulated factors of production are explained by the lack of important economic and political institutions such as a system assuring property rights and mechanisms for the efficient enforcement of contracts.

However, a key impediment may be an inability to take on larger, riskier projects and enjoy the high returns on investments. Following Acemoglu and Zilibotti (1997), a literature has asserted that the inability of poor countries to diversify risk combined with the indivisibility of many projects is the central explanation for the perverse phenomenon of both low growth and high volatility.[4] Figure 5.4 provides evidence in support of this view. Country growth rates of unit values are plotted with their variance through the 1990s. What emerges is a striking and statistically significant relationship between the two: Countries with riskier exports (measured by the standard deviation of unit values) enjoy higher growth of unit values. Perhaps more important, the poor countries are in the lower part of the risk-return profile. It is important to emphasize that this says nothing about the overall portfolio of exports, which also depends on the co-movements of unit values across goods. For example, richer countries may overall have a lower risk portfolio of exports. This issue will be dealt with in chapter 7.

This relationship continues to hold when the goods that countries export are controlled for. For instance, a rich country producing the same good as a poor country would still take on riskier investments and experience faster growth in quality. However, it appears that there is a strong risk-return profile in goods too. Here it is manufactures, particularly electronics and the like, that have the highest variance and natural resources that have the lowest. This stands in stark contrast with the stylized fact that natural resources have more volatile price movements. In fact, as discussed in chapters 2 and 7, it is the lack of diversification and not the intrinsic risks associated with these goods that drive that result. However, it also suggests that producing the higher risk goods is important for development.

The disaggregation into product and country effects is, at some level, less interesting than it first appears. In all likelihood, the same factors dictating that lower risk projects were taken on within goods are dictating that poor countries do not take on riskier goods.

What are these potential factors? The financial sector has emerged as central to diversifying these risks and supporting high rates of growth.

Figure 5.4 Growth and Standard Deviation of Quality Growth, 1990–2001
(Quantile regression)

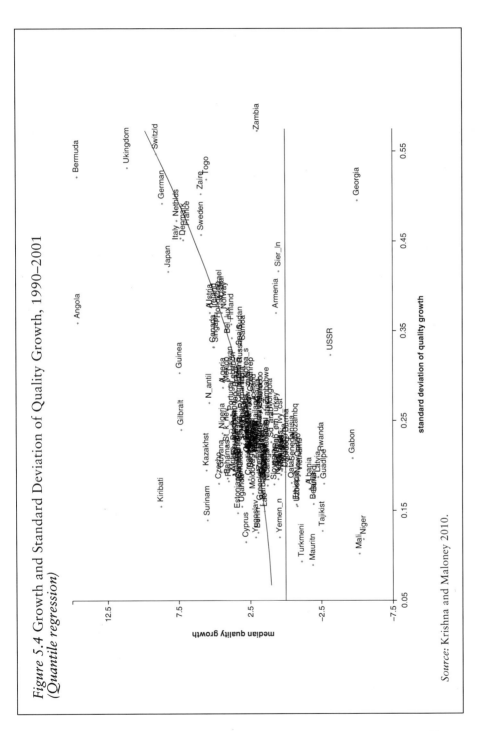

Source: Krishna and Maloney 2010.

Greenwood and Jovanovic (1990) argue that financial intermediates encourage high-yield investments and growth by performing dual roles: pooling idiosyncratic investment risks and eliminating ex-ante downside uncertainty about rates of return. Obstfeld (1994) sees international asset trade as encouraging all countries to shift from low-return, safe investments toward high-return, risky investments.

Grossman and Razin (1985) argue that multinational corporations may take on more risky production techniques within a country because they are more diversified internationally than local firms. In the area of trade, Baldwin (1989) argues that the differential ability of investors to diversify leads the country with better capital markets to export the "risky," and hence the higher return, good.[5] However, finance need not be the only barrier to countries taking on riskier projects. To the degree that Pasteur is right that "chance favors the prepared mind," an inability to resolve the well-known market failures and again, indivisibilities surrounding innovation and research and development would leave poorer countries restricted to less complex, and less risky products (for a recent application that emphasizes appropriation externalities over finance, see Hausmann, Hwang, and Rodrik 2007). Further, as Acemoglu, Johnson, and Robinson (2002) and Levchenko (2007) argue, weak supporting institutions that either exclude entrepreneurs, create additional uncertainty in the rules of the game, or make managing the implications of loss (for instance, bankruptcy laws) would also cause countries to specialize in lower risk goods. In the end, finance, barriers to research and development, and institutions are likely to be highly related.

To date, the evidence of these effects, although compelling, has been largely historical and anecdotal. For the 100 data points available here, financial depth, the degree of resolution of market failures in innovation, and institutional soundness, all when taken individually, influence a country's position on the risk-return frontier. However, in combined regressions that attempt to control for the strong correlations of these variables with development, the sample is severely restricted, and the correlations become less clear. Research and development emerges as the most robust proxy, although the data do not permit asserting that failures in the resolution of appropriation or other externalities are the principal or sole barrier for the emergence of high-risk exports with potential for fast unit value growth. Financial depth also enters, although less significantly, but is still viable as an explanation.

Thus far, we are tempted to conclude that national and industry-neutral policies might be preferred over the old style industrial policies that would demand that the public sector choose the high-risk, high-growth product to subsidize. However, it must also be acknowledged that such policies might have differential effects across products, as they would disproportionately stimulate the emergence of these types of products.

Entry and Exit Patterns

The preceding analysis has not taken into account the dynamic nature of the *composition* of regional export baskets. Quality may also increase with the introduction of new goods of higher relative quality. This section includes an analysis of the entry and exit patterns of goods in regional export baskets. "Entries" are composed of goods not traded from 1990 to 1995, and traded at least three times from 1996 to 2001. "Exits" are composed of goods traded at least three times from 1990 to 1995, and not traded from 1996 to 2001. "Incumbent" goods are goods traded at least three times in the 1990 to 95 period.

The median ratio of incoming to incumbent goods for the non-OECD regions is 1.03, and the median ratio for the OECD (high-income) countries is equal to 1.06. This implies that new goods enter at approximately the same level as existing goods within the region, but also that new goods enter at higher quality levels in richer countries than in poorer ones. At the upper end of the distribution, the quality ratio of entering to incumbent goods is larger for the non-OECD regions, suggesting a degree of convergence at the top end of the quality distribution between OECD and non-OECD countries.

Figure 5.5 disaggregates this by region, presenting the ratio at the 25th, 50th (median), and 75th percentiles. As compared with the previous results where there are roughly equal ratios of OECD (high-income) and non-OECD at the 50th percentile, important regional differences emerge. Compared to the OECD, Central Asia and the East Asia Pacific regions are 10 to 20 percent lower at the median, while Eastern Europe and South Asia are roughly 10 percent higher. The Latin America and the Caribbean region, the Middle East and North Africa region, and Sub-Saharan Africa are all roughly similar to the OECD at the 50th percentile level.

These counterintuitive findings are perhaps somewhat allayed by what is happening at the upper end of the distribution. Although both East Asia categories have lower median ratios, at the 75th quantile East Asia (high-income) equals that of the top performers. East Asia (low-income) is respectable as well. Arguably, the faster growing areas may have a broader distribution of exporters coming on line, many reflecting their relatively low average level of "caliber," but some being global superstars what are "leapfrogging." Eastern Europe stands out as having its entire distribution shifted right, with quantiles showing ratios 30–50 percent higher than the OECD. Since the period covered begins after the fall of the Berlin Wall in 1989, this may suggest that the pre-liberalization level of "caliber" or general technological sophistication could very broadly support goods of higher quality and some superstars, and that liberalization made this possible. Central Asia is largely shifted, or at least compressed left, and Africa is of a similar character, with modest median growth and no superstars.

Figure 5.5 Unit Value Ratio of New to Incumbent Goods
(25, 50, 75th percentiles)

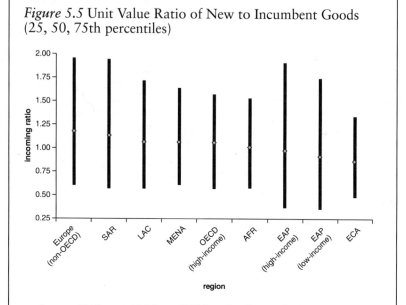

Sources: Krishna and Maloney (2011) and authors' calculations.
Note: AFR = Africa region; EAP = East Asia and the Pacific; ECA = Europe
and Central Asia; LAC = Latin America and the Caribbean region;
MENA = Middle East and North Africa region; OECD = Organisation for
Economic Co-operation and Development; SAR = South Asia region.

Micro-level work commissioned as background for this book broadly
confirms these patterns of entry and exit, and adds further complexity
to the dynamics. Lederman, Rodríguez-Clare, and Xu (2011) confirm
that in Costa Rica, new products enter at about 90 percent of the typical (median) incumbent basket. Alvarez and Fuentes (2009), using a rich
dataset of Chilean exporters during the period 1991–2001, identify four
stylized facts. First, every year a large number of new exporting relationships are initiated, but they represent a small share of the total value of
exports. Second, survival rates seem to be very low. After one year, around
one-quarter of new exporters are still exporting, but in the next year, only
about 12 percent retain the same status. This survival rate declines steadily
over time. Third, entry is generally associated with higher unit values.
This would be consistent with the idea that new exports are high-quality
products compared to incumbent export products. However, these quality
differences tend to decrease over time and eventually disappear three years
after entry. Fourth, there are significant differences across sectors and,
in particular, within sectors. Reference-price and differentiated products

show a higher price in the year of entry. It also takes longer for them to converge to the incumbent prices, whereas in the case of homogeneous goods, the new exporters enter with a higher price but rapidly converge to the price of the incumbents.

Conclusion

This chapter has examined export quality through the lens of the unit value. The literature documents a high degree of heterogeneity in prices even within very finely disaggregated goods. On average, this measure of "quality" rises with level of development. Therefore, the dynamics of unit values offers a window on broader development issues.

The chapter finds that there is a convergence dynamic, that is, within a good, countries further from the frontier will, all things being equal, experience faster growth rates of their export unit values. In this sense, Latin America, for instance, is at a bit of a disadvantage in its concentration in commodities, which tend to have shorter quality (unit value) ladders. Further, there is evidence that goods matter. Many manufactures appear to offer greater opportunities for investments that will yield more rapid growth in quality.

In this context, two observations can be made. First, what is not clear is that there is a market failure that would dictate that the Latin American and Caribbean economies should be specialized in goods that defy their comparative advantage in commodities. Lower possibilities for unit value growth may translate into lower profitability, but there is no obvious externality that the market cannot see and which must be corrected. Moving into other noncommodity goods against a country's comparative advantage will likely involve welfare losses.

Second, and critically related to the previous point, the findings indicate that the convergence effects are swamped by idiosyncratic regional factors which make the OECD (high-income) continue to grow relatively faster, even controlling for goods. Even if the Latin America and the Caribbean region had the OECD basket of goods, it would perform much worse. This again points to the "how" and not just the "what" of export decisions, although as of now one can only speculate on the factors undermining the region's performance. However, numerous behind-the-border factors, such as the resolution of market failures in technology, the depth of financial markets, and the quality of institutions, appear to be relevant. Further, the literature has put an emphasis on human capital accumulation generally as a key promoter of quality.[6] These factors not only affect the quality growth within a good category, but also are likly to affect what goods are produced, and, in particular, whether a country produces those with the greatest potential for quality growth. Hence, it seems that national sector-neutral policies can help development precisely because they may have disproportionately positive effects on riskier goods that appear to experience fast growth rates in unit values.

Notes

1. See Brooks (2006), Hallak and Schott (2008), Kugler and Verhoogen (2008) and Khandelwal (2010) have argued that additional information on the relative demand for products needs to be incorporated to make true quality comparisons. For purposes here, the assumption is that, on average, the raw unit values capture differences in quality, albeit with measurement error.

2. This is consistent with Bustos (2010) who added a measure of technological choice to the Melitz framework. Bustos found that, for Argentina, reduction of import tariffs by its *Mercado Común del Sur* (MERCOSUR) or Common Southern Market partners increased both the probability of firm entry into these export markets and spending on technology.

3. Relatedly, Brambilla, Lederman, and Porto (2012) find that Argentine manufacturing firms paid higher average wages and hired more skilled workers upon shifting their exports from Brazil to high-income markets (the United States and Europe) during the Brazilian devaluation of 1999. These changes in skill utilization by firms were associated with exports with higher unit value variances than other exports.

4. Do and Levchenko (2007) also postulate a model in which financial services are endogenous and countries producing low-finance-intensive goods will have financial markets that cannot support taking on more risky goods. A related literature is reviewed, and the empirical validity of the Acemoglu and Zilibotti (1997) theory is in chapter 7 of this book.

5. The association of increasingly complex or involved products suggests that the diversification channel need not be the only financial barrier, and that barriers need not, in fact, originate in the financial sector. Bardan and Kletzer (1987) argue that more sophisticated manufactured finished products require more credit to cover selling and distribution costs than primary or intermediate products. Therefore, imperfections in credit markets, even where technology and endowments are identical, can lead to specialization of countries with higher levels of sovereign risk or imperfect domestic credit markets in less sophisticated products. Beck (2002) builds a model in which manufacturing, due to exhibiting increasing returns to scale, is more finance intensive due to increasing returns to scale.

6. In a paper commissioned for this study, Waugh (2008) offers a general equilibrium theory of the supply and demand for product quality, and international trade that sees quality as an important feature to understanding bilateral trade volumes. He argues that intermediate goods are available in different quality and this quality is complementary to domestic human capital: Skilled workers are better able to use higher quality intermediate goods. Higher human capital countries are able to produce all levels of quality for export, whereas poor countries can produce only those at the lower end of the spectrum. Introducing quality in his simulations, he is able to replicate up to 75 percent of the observed variation in the volume of bilateral trade compared to the model, with no quality considerations.

6

Heterogeneity in the Production of Goods

The previous chapter explored the extraordinary variation in the "quality" of goods within even very fine levels of disaggregation. This chapter will continue exploring additional dimensions of heterogeneity that further reflect that it is likely to be as important how a country produces even a very commodity-type product, as the product itself. More fundamentally, it is possible to conclude that much of the time even very finely categorized exports can represent very different steps in the global production process. Therefore, placing the notion of the "good" at the center of the policy discussion may be greatly misleading.

How Things Are Produced Matters

In some sense, much of the economic literature sees the process of development as the progressively more efficient production of the archetypal widget. Hence, the notion that a good can be produced in many different ways is not at all alien. But its importance for the present discussion cannot be overstated.

The Chilean historical experience with exporting copper is illustrative. In 1870, Chile was the world's largest producer. Yet by 1904, output had fallen in absolute terms to the point where there was a question about whether the industry could survive. As occurred in Mexico, the mines were then largely bought by foreigners, particularly from the United States, and Chilean participation became negligible. Today, fortunes have reversed and the Chilean national company, the National Copper Corporation of Chile (CODELCO), is a major global player. This reversal cannot be a function of the good because copper has not changed that much. However, it has everything to do with the Chilean ability to bring new technologies into production at different historical periods. At the turn of the 20th century, Chile lacked the innovative capacity to employ new technologies and, in particular, the Bessemer process and new applications of electrolysis.

By contrast, Wright uses the same U.S. experience with copper as an example of how nations learn: It developed a knowledge industry with a network of expertise which, in addition to allowing the Americans to profitably take over Chilean copper production, also laid the foundation for expansion into other fields of engineering and manufacturing. It was the same product but produced with a completely different outcome (see Maloney 2007). Hence, in *Natural Resources: Neither Curse nor Destiny,* Lederman and Maloney (2007) argue that the huge historical variation in development experience based on natural resources suggests that it is more fruitful to investigate the variation than the "average" tendency and notions of a "conditional curse" move in this direction. How countries leverage their resources is as important as the resource endowments themselves.

Smart Goods or Smart Production Processes?

This lesson extends far beyond the natural resource issue to all types of goods. The American and Chilean examples with copper suggest that virtually identical goods can be produced at very different levels of sophistication and with very distinct long-run impacts on growth. There is suggestive evidence that this is also true today within goods often thought to be "high-tech" manufactured goods. These are often thought to be knowledge industries with the potential for spillovers. However, again, whether or not such spillovers occur depends importantly on how these goods are produced.

As a crude measure of whether such high-tech goods actually lead to knowledge generation and learning, is revealing to consider the degree of patenting. Figure 6.1 shows the Index of Revealed Comparative Advantage in Innovation (IRCAI) in the production of Mexican computers and Brazilian aircraft (Lederman and Maloney 2006). This is the number of Mexican patents given in a particular sector over the total number of Mexican patents, divided by the global analogue. If Mexico, with a large computer sector, is producing relatively more patents in this sector than is the case globally, the IRCAI >1, then it has an innovation comparative advantage in the sector.

However, this is not the case for Mexico. For a 20-year period, Mexico has shown a comparative disadvantage (less than 1) in innovation (as measured by patents) in the sector. Where this country trades more is not where it innovates more. A similar finding emerges for aircraft in Brazil. In neither case is it easy to argue that any knowledge cluster in these countries corresponds to its largest exports. By contrast, the Republic of Korea (not shown) has moved from a position below that of Mexico to an IRCAI above 3.

Figure 6.1 is not encouraging for these large Latin American economies in the sense that industries that could be deemed sophisticated or "high tech" and in which these countries have developed a presence in export markets do not seem to be the source of much innovation. However, more recent data can be used to assess more generally the relationship between comparative advantage in trade and innovation, as well as the relationship between export market share and the patent market share. Perhaps there is no relationship, in which case to speak of manufacturing industries (such as computers, electronics, and aircraft) as being somehow superior in terms of their potential for providing knowledge spillovers or in protecting rents emanating from the expected innovation with patents, might not make much economic sense.

Figures 6.2a–6.2c show scatter plots of indexes of the revealed comparative advantage in trade (considering both exports and imports, as in

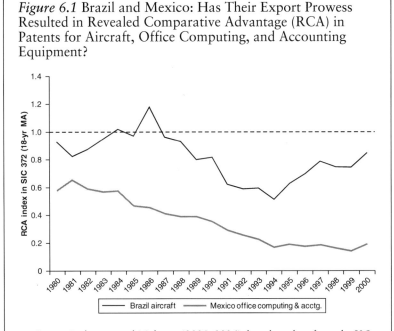

Figure 6.1 Brazil and Mexico: Has Their Export Prowess Resulted in Revealed Comparative Advantage (RCA) in Patents for Aircraft, Office Computing, and Accounting Equipment?

Source: Lederman and Maloney (2005, 2006), based on data from the U.S. Patent and Trademark Office and its Standard Industrial Classification (SIC) of patents of 2000.

Figures 6.2a–c Revealed Comparative Advantage (RCA) in
Exports versus RCA in Innovation (1980–2005)

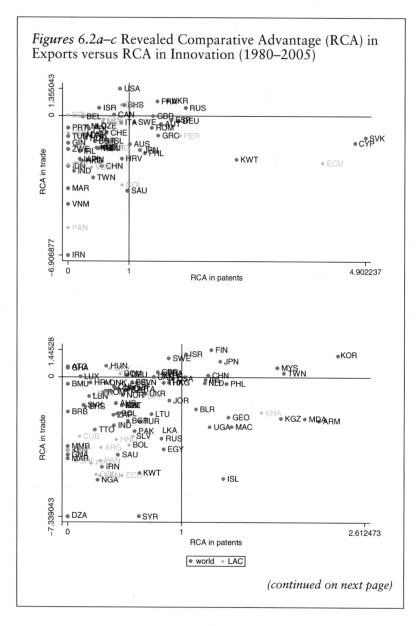

(continued on next page)

Vollrath 1991) and patents. The latter varies between zero and infinity.
The vertical and horizontal lines cutting through these graphs indicate
the level of comparative advantage. For example, a value greater than
zero in trade indicates comparative advantage in trade, and a value
greater than one in patents suggests comparative advantage in patenting.

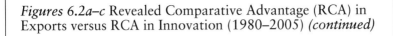

Figures 6.2a–c Revealed Comparative Advantage (RCA) in Exports versus RCA in Innovation (1980–2005) *(continued)*

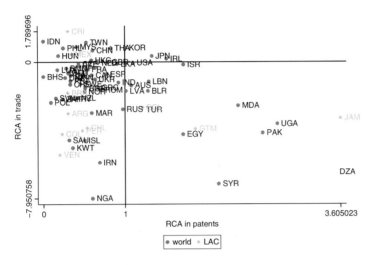

Source: Authors' calculations

Note: "Index of Revealed Comparative Advantage in Innovation (IRCAI) calculated using patents from U.S. PTO (1963–2004). Revealed Comparative Advantage in trade (RCA) calculated using U.N. COMTRADE (1980–2005) as described in text. Sectors: Aircraft (SIC 372), Electronics (SIC 366), Computers (SIC 357).

Therefore, countries in the upper right quadrant have a comparative advantage in both; those in the lower left quadrant have neither. The data on trade cover the period 1980–2004, and the patent data cover 1963–2004. Using the same data (but not on imports), figures 6.3a–6.3c show the relationship between country rankings in export market shares and patenting shares by sector. The economies of Latin America and the Caribbean are differentiated from the rest of the global samples in both sets of graphs.

The findings about revealed comparative advantage in trade versus innovation tell a consistent story for the three sectors: The regional powerhouses in trade for each one of these potentially "high-tech" industries do not appear to have developed a corresponding comparative advantage in innovation. In the case of aircraft, Brazil appears in the upper left quadrant, indicating comparative advantage in trade but not in patenting.[1] Likewise, in the case of electronics only Mexico and the Dominican Republic appear to have a comparative advantage in trade. However, neither managed to develop an industry with innovation potential.[2] Finally, the last graph in this series shows that neither Costa Rica nor Mexico developed an innovation-based computer industry, despite their stellar trade performance in this sector. Costa Rica, in fact, has received zero patents in this sector since 1997, the year when INTEL Corporation began its operations. Hence, the regional experience suggests that it is difficult to argue that comparative advantage in a high-tech-sounding industry is synonymous with a knowledge industry.

The How

In the cases of both Chilean copper and the aircraft, electronics, and computer industries, there is evidence that goods can be produced in very different ways and with very different results. Indeed, the literature suggests that the phenomenon is more general. Blomström and Kokko (2007) demonstrate the sophistication of the Swedish forestry industry to be far higher than that of Chile or Brazil. Wright and Czelusta (2007) discuss "mineral underperformers" to describe Latin America's low-productivity, low-exploration mining enterprises. At a very aggregate level, Martin and Mitra (2001) also find by using simple total factor productivity regressions that differential rates of productivity growth exist within manufactures and agriculture by country. Developing countries, on average, show lower rates of growth in both manufactures and agriculture.

Combined with the findings of dramatic variance in the quality from the previous chapter, two important conclusions can be drawn and one open policy question can be raised. First, both the quality of very finely disaggregated goods and the way in which even very homogeneous goods are produced can vary greatly according to country context. Second, the fact that a country produces a particular good does not guarantee that whatever positive things may be associated with that good will appear in that context. Countries do not automatically become the best of what they produce.

The open policy question, then, is how can the development impact of whatever basket is produced be maximized (including leveraging it into new products)? What are the complementary actions that countries need to take, and might these be more important than what is actually produced?

As noted previously, Wright documents how the United States leveraged copper extraction into a major knowledge network by incorporating higher level human capital, universities, and private sector firms that both led to the invention of new techniques for copper processing and laid the foundation for moving into new industries. Blomström and Kokko (2007) argue the same for the Nordic forestry industries. Table 6.1 shows just one set of institutions involved in the pulp and paper cluster in Sweden. The agglomeration of high-level research in states and institutions for the development of human capital is far beyond what would be found in Chile or Brazil today.

These findings also explain how a forestry company in Finland with a cellulose mill at the town of Nokia would become a major telecommunications giant, or how a Finnish copper company would become Outokumpu, one of the world's largest producers of fine tolerance stainless steel products—while neither of these transformations occurred in Latin America. Forestry and copper were cultivated as very knowledge-intensive industries such that, to use Wright's phrase, the companies

Table 6.1 Participants in the Knowledge and Skill Cluster in the Paper and Pulp Industry (1990)

	Generation	Dissemination
Skills (Education)	Royal Technical University	Swedish Pulp and Paper Research Institute
	Chalmers Technical University	
	University of Karlstad	
	Swedish Pulp and Paper Research Institute	
Knowledge (Research)	Royal Technical University	Swedish Pulp and Paper Research Institute
	Chalmers Technical University	Institute of Surface Chemistry Graphical Research Laboratory
	University of Karlstad	Swedish Packaging Research Institute
	Swedish Pulp and Paper Research Institute	Swedish Newspaper Mills' Research Laboratory
	Institute of Surface Chemistry Graphical Research Laboratory	
	Swedish Packaging Research Institute	
	Swedish Newspaper Mills' Research Laboratory	

Sources: Blomström and Kokko (2007) and Lederman and Maloney (2007).

and the countries as a whole "learned how to learn." The essentiality of this embrace of knowledge as complementary to factor endowments is central to Lederman and Maloney's (2007) treatment of the natural resource success stories and the failures in Latin America. But it extends to all goods.

Returning to chapter 3, the monkey-tree argument could be recast to say that it is not how close the trees are but the quality of the monkeys, and whether they have the capacity to learn and jump to new levels of sophistication or quality, and new industries. Put differently, even if Volvo had not yet been invented, is it likely that Chile's forestry industry would somehow generate it? Are Chilean or Brazilian monkeys as good at jumping among trees as their Swedish counterparts, with a vastly deeper engineering tradition and generally far higher human capital? As Blomström and Kokko (2006) argue, what made Nokia possible was that it came from an innovative company, not that it came from a company producing a certain good. The Scandinavian forestry sectors trained very adept monkeys who could identify and, especially, create new trees.

Goods or Tasks?

The variation in performance across countries points to a larger issue that affects virtually all discussions about desirable export baskets. Because two countries' trade statistics register that they export a particular good does not, in fact, mean that they are engaged in the same activity. In the era of globalized production where production is fragmented and allocated among distinct countries, different segments of the production process are produced by different countries. The findings about different production technologies and differing degrees of knowledge generation in the computing industry, for example, may be driven not by differing production processes, but rather by the fact that countries like Mexico are simply providing a last stage of a production process that is, in fact, not the one associated with skilled labor or patenting. Producing the last assembly stage of computers may appear as exporting high-tech goods in the trade statistics, but fundamentally, the value added being exported derives from unskilled labor that could just as well be employed in assembling shoes.

Fundamentally, rather than talking about trade in goods, the focus should be on trade in tasks. This question is nowhere clearer than in the electronic manufacturing goods that have become icons of the current Chinese miracle. Box 6.1 suggests that although China exports the iPod to the United States, only 1 percent of the value added it generates accrues to China. This suggests a need to look closer at the actual contribution that China is making to the production process relative to, for instance, that of Apple Inc.

Box 6.1 Who Makes the iPod?

Each import of a finished iPod into the United States contributes roughly US$150 to the China–U.S. bilateral trade deficit. Frequently, this kind of product is considered a desirable "high-tech" product with likely high knowledge spillovers.

Yet in this era of extraordinarily fragmented production processes and extended value chains, how much really accrues to China? Following the value added requires information not easily available, but Linden, Kraemer, and Dedrick (2009) conclude that it is not very much.

Of the US$299 retail price in the United States, US$163 was captured by U.S. companies and workers; US$75 went for distribution and retail; US$80 went to Apple for its invention and overall coordination of production; and US$8 went to various component makers. Japan earned about US$26 through the Toshiba disk drive. In the end, only a handful of dollars or just above 1 percent of the value added of the iPod accrued to China's labor for what is largely assembly work.

Source: Linden, Kraemer, and Dedrick (2009). See also Kraemer, Linden, and Dedrick (2011) on the iPad and iPhone.

An emerging literature in international trade on the implications of such a shift in emphasis toward tasks and fragmentation has developed. (See, for example, Grossman and Rossi-Hansberg 2006, 2008; Antràs, Garicano, and Rossi-Hansberg 2006; and Baldwin and Robert-Nicoud 2010.) A whole new set of issues arises, of which only a few of the most relevant will be explored below.

First, exporting "high-tech" goods may say nothing about whether the skills employed are somehow correspondingly "high tech." To use the terminology of chapter 4, countries may get the dumb or simpler part of the production of "smart" goods. As Goh Keng Swee, Singapore's one-time Minister of Finance (1970), commented, "the electronic components we make in Singapore require less skill than that required by barbers or cooks, involving mostly repetitive manual operations"[3] The recent Chinese experience too, suggests that the vast exports of electronics are, in fact, exports of unskilled assembly work. And, as Kobrin (2007) argues, the possible spillovers expected from producing certain goods are reduced as only specific assembly tasks are transferred. He suggests that core-periphery arguments may gain in relevance as a result.

Second, these segments of the production chain have become so standardized and the barriers to entry so low that they have been termed "commodity manufactures." (See, for example, Breznitz and Murphree 2011.) Again, looking at the demand side of the equation, the competition even among Chinese firms drives the margins down to the barest minimum. As noted by Steinfeld (2004), the emphasis on standardized, non differentiated products offers little alternative but to compete on the basis of low cost and high volume. Moreover, firms continually run the risk of being unseated by the next low-cost entrant, locking firms into a mutually destructive price competition.

Clearly, high-tech exports in this context are not "high value added" in any sense of the word. Figure 6.3, at a very aggregate level, shows that electronic products have only 22 percent value added while some other low PRODY goods, such as coking, furniture, or chemical products, have much higher. (Interestingly, any positive slope is driven by natural resource products exported by rich countries, such as nonmetallic mineral products.) Disaggregating further, table 6.2 shows that electronics and other "high-tech" products are at the bottom of the domestic value-added list. Computers contribute only 4.6 percent. At the high end are a variety of natural resource and industrial "basics" such as chemical fertilizers, metal processing, and the like. The development impact of a unit gain in productivity is going to be larger in these goods. Hence, when the literature talks about "moving into high value added products," it needs to be more precise. For China this would imply moving out of computers and into hemp textiles.

The findings indicate that the focus should be on moving up to higher value-added tasks. But again, there is little evidence that there is an automatic progression up the value chain or toward greater value added along other dimensions. As Breznitz and Murphree (2011) argue, even for domestically completed goods for domestic consumption, after licenses and fees for the use for foreign technology, China can feel trapped at the lowest value added of final state assemblers. Much of the present discussion around the Chinese drive for indigenous innovation and indifferent enforcement of intellectual property rights relates precisely to China's goal of moving from a model of "Made in China" to "Innovated in China" (Segal 2010; Breznitz and Murphrees 2011).

Thus, from a conceptual point of view, the final export product becomes very misleading as a measure of desirability of the activity actually being undertaken. As Steinfeld (2004, 1972–1973) notes in his work on China's "shallow" integration into the global production chain:

[W]hether for aerospace or apparel, we can conceive of some activities within their respective industry supply chains that are standardized and commodified, and other activities that are highly proprietary, as yet utterly uncodifiable, and highly lucrative. We can also see that as different firms occupy different parts of the supply chain—whether in high-tech industries or low, capital intensive or non-intensive—some of those firms will occupy high-value activities for which knowledge is embedded and sustainable competitive

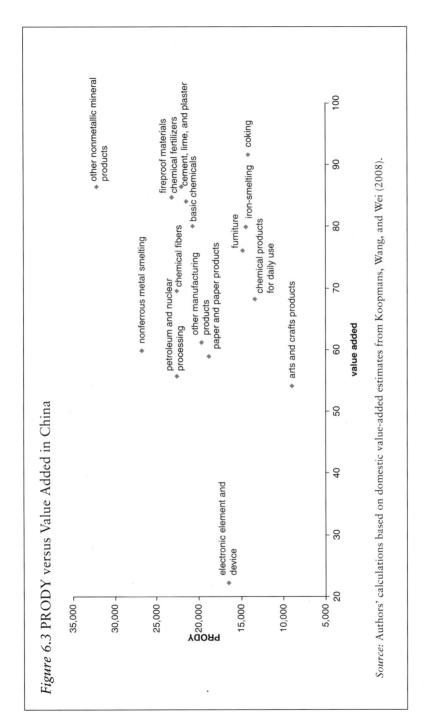

Figure 6.3 PRODY versus Value Added in China

Source: Authors' calculations based on domestic value-added estimates from Koopmans, Wang, and Wei (2008).

Table 6.2 China: 10 Exports with the Lowest Domestic
Value Added (% of exports)

Electronics/computers	4.6
Telecommunication equipment	14.9
Cultural and office equipment	19.1
Other computer peripheral equipment	19.7
Electronic elements and devices	22.2
Radio, television, and communication equipment	35.5
Household electric appliances	37.2
Plastic products	37.4
Generators	39.6
Instruments, meters, and other measuring equipment	42.2
China: 10 Exports with the Highest Domestic Value Added	
Agriculture, forestry, animal husbandry, and fishing machinery	81.8
Hemp textiles	82.7
Metalworking machinery	83.4
Steel pressing	83.4
Pottery, china, and earthenware	83.4
Chemical fertilizers	84.0
Fireproof materials	84.7
Cement, lime, and plaster	86.4
Other nonmetallic mineral products	86.4
Coking	91.6

Source: Koopmans, Wang, and Wei (2008).

advantage is possible, while other firms will not, instead delegated
to standardized activities for which competition is intense, churning
significant, and returns decidedly low....

...Whereas in previous decades, the entrance of Mexican or Chinese firms into the steel, automotive or machine-building sectors
would have itself been understood as signifying upgrading—simply
by virtue of entrance into ostensibly higher-tech, knowledge-intensive industries—our focus today on particular activities, and the
ability to distinguish those that are modular from those that are
integral in any supply chain, forces us to think more precisely about
exactly which activities really do constitute upgrading and which do

not, which activities accord sustainable competitive advantage and growth, and which do not.

The observation that the appropriate focus should be on the type of value added being contributed by the country rather than the good as it appears on the export ledgers goes beyond efforts to classify goods by level of development of exporters (PRODY), or level of high technology. All the discussion to this point around characteristics inherent to goods should ideally be discussed in the context of specific tasks that may or may not be unique to a particular good. Given the absence of analysis in anything but anecdotal form about which tasks may lead to more rapid development, policy makers are again left with little in the way of guidance on which path should be encouraged or discouraged. And again, how a country approaches these tasks may be as or more important.

To modify the previous conclusion, it may not be which task is undertaken per se, but rather how it is done and even more, how countries can build on it. For instance, are there proprietary production skills, intellectual assets, and the like that would permit some quasi-rents and freedom from competition? It may be that what is needed is the establishment of a playing field that will support the production of goods in line with comparative advantage *and* facilitate developing the factors of production that will allow for diversification into progressively more attractive tasks. One can start from a position that allows some rents, natural resources perhaps, or simply the application of cutting-edge manufacturing techniques to a very low wage workforce. However, how these tasks are built upon will determine their ultimate impact on development. This seems to be on the minds of Chinese policy makers. By contrast, the "Innovated in Latin America" slogan has yet to be clearly heard and the issue of "how" the tasks are engaged in does not yet appear high on the regional agenda.

Notes

1. The regional observation in this graph with the small-numbers problem and in the lower right quadrant is St. Kitts and Nevis from the Caribbean.
2. The two Latin America and Caribbean economies with comparative advantage in aircraft patents are Peru and Ecuador, which patented so little during 1963–2004 that a tiny number of patents assigned to this sector appear as having contributed a huge share of total patents. This small-numbers problem appears in the other sector graphs as well.
3. (Goh 1972, 275) *The Economics of Modernization and Other Essays.* Cited in Alwyn Young 2002. "A Tale of Two Cities: Factor Accumulation and Technical Change in Hong Kong and Singapore."

7

Trade Quality as Portfolio Diversification

Previous chapters discussed notions of trade quality related to the types and prices (or unit values) of exported products. However tempting it might be to focus industrial and other policies solely on the development of specific products or sectors, such policies can change the overall pattern of trade, which itself might affect national welfare and growth prospects. This chapter reflects this view of the quality of trade, emphasizing the overall distribution of export revenues across all potential export products.

When the overall distribution of export revenues is considered as a policy objective, it becomes clear that traditional notions of industrial policy might be outdated. The slogan "picking winners" becomes more than a challenge for the foresight of central planners with good intentions; it becomes a potentially harmful approach that could increase rather than decrease export concentration.

With the aim of clarifying various challenges related to traditional industrial policies focused on specific goods or sectors, this chapter analyzes how development can be viewed as a process of economic diversification. In turn, the chapter briefly revisits potential market failures that could justify public interventions to stimulate private sector investments in product innovation and diversification. The discussion reviews the main theoretical arguments, but also acknowledges that the evidence on market failures is indirect at best.

A second tour of the so-called "curse of natural resources" through the lens of export concentration is also warranted. The concern that concomitant export concentration could affect economic welfare through macroeconomic volatility will be addressed. New empirical evidence is briefly discussed, followed by a survey of the emerging literature on how export concentration can be seen as an outcome of volatility, focusing on the role of exchange-rate volatility as a determinant of the composition of exports, with important policy implications.

The chapter concludes with discussions about two broad policy questions: (1) Can industrial policies correctly choose winning export products? (2) Should such policies focus on narrow sectors? The evidence presented in this chapter can support certain types of industrial policies, namely, interventions that focus on portfolio diversification of exports, but also orthodox policies related to financial market development, trade liberalization, and other reforms that can reduce barriers to the emergence of exportable products.

Development as Diversification

The seminal article by Imbs and Wacziarg (2003) analyzes the process of diversification across income levels. The data on production and employment concentration across countries gathered by these authors suggest a robust pattern whereby economic diversification increases with the level of development, until reaching a relatively high level of GDP per capita, after which time economies become increasingly specialized. This finding is provocative as it contradicts a basic tenet of neoclassical trade models, which predict that specialization produces improvements in economic efficiency and ultimately development.

Klinger and Lederman (2004, 2006, 2011) were among the first to study the empirical relationship between diversification, export-product discoveries, and the level of development. Unlike the exponentially positive trajectory of patenting activity, export discoveries tend to peak at a low level of income per capita, and fall monotonically with development thereafter. The Imbs-Wacziarg U-shape function of concentration is apparent in the trade data; diversification peaks around $20,000 purchasing power parity (PPP) and declines thereafter.[1]

Market Failures in Product Innovation and Diversification

Numerous models in the literature suggest that market failures inhibit the discovery process, thereby constraining diversification and possibly development. In the words of Harrison and Rodríguez-Clare (2010, 4041), "... just as research and development subsidies are appropriate responses to innovation spillovers, policies to promote entry into new industries are appropriate to deal with information spillovers associated with the discovery of new profitable activities."

One such model is Hausmann and Rodrik's model of "Economic Development as Self-Discovery" (2003). This model suggests that although factor endowments explain broad patterns of production across countries, production functions for goods at a disaggregated level are not known a priori. However, once an entrepreneur has an experiment that pays off and "discovers" a profitable product, others can easily imitate that success, free-riding on the initial investments in experimentation and thereby driving down the entrepreneur's profits by lowering the price of the good (if the country is a large exporter relative to the global market) or by raising the costs of production (when production requires nontradable inputs or factors of production). The result is a market failure, whereby entrepreneurs are not able to reap the full benefits of their discovery investment, and they will consequently under invest in experimentation. There is social value in discovering what can be produced in each country setting, yet competition can lead to underinvestment in the experimentation required to make these discoveries. In this context, there is scope for public intervention.

Vettas (2000) suggested another model with uncertain demand, which must be discovered. Furthermore, foreign demand is itself an increasing function of past sales due to learning on the part of consumers (up to a maximum point, which is not predictable a priori). However, the initial investment required to penetrate a new market, stimulate demand, and learn the market's potential size will suffer from the same appropriability problem: Imitators can free ride, leading to underinvestment in demand discovery by entrepreneurs, thereby justifying public subsidies for entry into new markets.

Based on a similar argument of free-riding on market-cultivating expenditures, originally advanced by Bhagwati (1968), Mayer (1984) presents a model of foreign market cultivation that assumes actual consumption experiences are required to learn about a commodity's qualities. The model indicates that subsidization of infant-exporters is a first-best policy. Another extension relates to foreign standards, as in Ganslandt and Markusen (2000). When attempting to export a good to a foreign market, the first entrant will have to make the initial investments in product and process redesign to meet foreign product safety standards. However, market failures will arise if redesigns are non excludable, as free-riding will reduce the returns of the first entrant.

Scarce Evidence of Market Failures

Although interesting, these models have not been subjected to systematic empirical testing. This is likely due, in part, to a lack of disaggregated worldwide production data, combined with no obvious method for the testing of the presence of these market failures. Some recent research has attempted to identify market failures in product innovation indirectly by studying how competition affects product innovation according to countries or firms.

Klinger and Lederman (2006, 2011) study how the profitability of exports interacts with barriers to entry in shaping the probability of export-product innovation within sectors across countries. Their results, which are robust to various specifications controlling for country-specific effects among other variables, suggest that for a given rate of export growth, the probability of product innovation *increases* with barriers to entry (proxied by the standard indicators from the *Doing Business* database). This counterintuitive result can be interpreted as evidence of market failures: If there were no appropriability problem, then barriers to entry should be associated with lower rather than higher probabilities of export-product discoveries.

Another indirect test of the existence of market failures is related to how firms react to the activities of their domestic competitors. If innovation by others leads to firm innovation, then it is possible that social benefits of product innovation by a firm can exceed the private benefits. Lederman (2010) studies product innovation by firms with data from 68 countries, covering more than 25,000 firms in eight manufacturing sectors. The author assesses the predictions of interdisciplinary research on innovation by firms. The econometric evidence suggests that globalization and local knowledge (proxied by the accumulated stock of patents granted to local inventors) increase the likelihood that firms will introduce new products. By contrast, domestic regulatory impediments to competition are not robustly correlated with product innovation. Both trade liberalization and innovation effort (at the country level) seem to promote product innovation by incumbent firms. However, barriers to firm entry are unrelated to product innovation, on average.

Harrison and Rodríguez-Clare (2010, 4041) discuss the theoretical merits of various types of market failures for justifying trade protection (which are never first best; direct subsidies are). They ask the ever-enduring question about policy effectiveness: "While a number of market failures could justify government intervention in theory, one key question is whether IP [industrial policy] has worked in practice." We address this question in a novel, albeit indirect, approach, which is consistent with the notion of quality of trade being related to the overall concentration of trade.

Natural Resources, Export Concentration, and Volatility

Lederman and Maloney (2007) point out that the curse of natural resources could be a myth. Of particular relevance is their finding that the most robustly negatively correlated indicator of natural resource exports with economic growth is the share of natural resource exports in total merchandise exports. Lederman and Maloney (2008) subsequently showed that this indicator is not a good theoretical proxy for the *abundance* of natural resources. Rather, it is a measure of export concentration. In the cross-country growth regressions presented in Lederman and Maloney (2007), the curse vanishes after controlling for the Herfindahl Index of export concentration. If export concentration is associated with macroeconomic volatility, as will be analyzed below, then it is possible that countries might face a curse of concentration rather than a curse of natural resources per se. Even if macroeconomic volatility does not directly affect economic growth, for a given rate of income or consumption growth, volatility dampens social welfare.

Here we study the correlates of macroeconomic volatility and assess the validity of two complementary hypotheses:

(i) Commodity dependence can exacerbate macroeconomic uncertainty through a *structural* channel whereby export concentration leads to terms-of-trade volatility. This is then manifested as volatility of the growth of income or consumption per capita. This hypothesis is consistent with the well-known literature on the "Dutch Disease," whereby natural resource discoveries (booms) are associated with general equilibrium effects (price and income effects) that reduce the size of the tradable sector, which has traditionally been associated with a process of deindustrialization (see, for example, Corden and Neary 1982).

(ii) Commodity dependence is associated with institutional weaknesses that make *governments incapable of managing external volatility.* Thus, commodity-dependent economies can experience a pronounced transmission of terms-of-trade volatility into income and consumption volatility. This hypothesis is consistent with the so-called "voracity effect" created by natural resource windfalls, which has been associated with the worsening of public institutions (Lane and Tornell 1999).

A first look at the data is not conclusive, especially for the sample of Latin American and Caribbean economies. Table 7.1 contains the necessary descriptive statistics. It shows volatility indicators, namely, the standard deviation of the annual growth of each variable from 1980 to 2005. It also shows the average external prices (export, import, and terms-of-trade indexes, which are weighted averages of unit values of exports and imports). In addition, it contains volatility indicators for real (PPP adjusted) GDP and consumption per capita, as well as for various potential covariates of macroeconomic volatility, including trade openness, financial development, and rule of law (as a proxy of the quality of public institutions).

Table 7.1 Natural Resources, Macroeconomic Volatility, and Trade Concentration, 1980–2005

	Global sample		Latin America and Caribbean (LAC)		Latin American and Caribbean net exporters of energy and mining		Other net exporters of energy and mining	
	Obs.	Mean	Obs.	Mean	Obs.	Mean	Obs.	Mean
Volatility Indicators								
Export price index	139	0.132	19	0.133	15	0.122	59	0.151
Import price index	139	0.113	19	0.112	15	0.098	59	0.117
Terms of trade	139	0.091	19	0.094	15	0.088	59	0.110
GDP per capita	155	0.059	21	0.043	14	0.040	70	0.071
Other Variables								
Net exports of mining per worker	150	0.375	21	0.091	15	0.171	63	1.200
Net exports of agriculture per worker	151	0.087	22	0.172	15	0.263	63	0.412
Export concentration	153	0.321	22	0.313	15	0.297	65	0.405
Import concentration	155	0.137	22	0.128	15	0.117	67	0.134
Trade over GDP in 1980	109	63.634	20	52.066	15	48.797	50	68.611
Private credit over GDP in 1980	107	30.979	21	27.528	15	24.733	47	25.720
Rule of law index in 1982–84	118	3.072	22	2.359	15	2.493	54	2.994

Source: Authors' calculations based on data from the World Bank, International Monetary Fund, and United Nations Commercial and Trade Statistics (UNCOMTRADE).

Notes: GDP = gross domestic product; Obs = number of observations. Export and import concentration are measured by the root of the Herfindahl index.

The first two columns contain the data from the global sample, followed by the data from Latin America and the Caribbean. The last six columns show the corresponding statistics for the sample of Latin American and Caribbean and non-Latin-American net exporters of mining and energy commodities. The data show that all Latin American and Caribbean net exporters of mining and energy were also net exporters of agricultural commodities during 1980–2005.

The data do not support the view that the Latin America and the Caribbean region or its exporters of natural resources suffered from unusually high external volatility. In contrast, non-Latin-American net exporters of mining and energy did, in fact, face higher export and import price volatility than the global and Latin American samples. This group of countries also had export structures that were significantly more concentrated. Partly because the descriptive statistics are inconclusive, it is necessary to assess the validity of the hypotheses linking natural resource dependence and volatility with multivariate econometric estimations.

Figure 7.1 illustrates the relationship between merchandise export-revenue concentration and terms-of-trade volatility. The positive

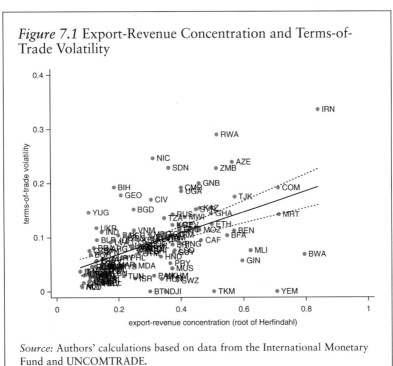

Figure 7.1 Export-Revenue Concentration and Terms-of-Trade Volatility

Source: Authors' calculations based on data from the International Monetary Fund and UNCOMTRADE.
Note: Dotted lines represent the 5 percent confidence interval.

correlation between these variables appears to be strong, although it does not hold in the previous comparison between Latin American net exporters of energy and mining and the overall sample of countries from the region.

We consider econometric estimates, focusing on the issue of endogeneity, although the results seem to be robust to the inclusion of a plethora of control variables, including import concentration, financial development, institutions (proxied by law and order), the ratio of trade over GDP, and even GDP per capita, among other controls.[2]

Table 7.2 presents the econometric estimates. These estimates simultaneously explore the determinants of merchandise export-revenue concentration, terms-of-trade volatility, and GDP-per-capita growth volatility. The model of export concentration suggests that it is positively correlated with net exports of energy and mining commodities, but negatively correlated with net exports of agricultural products. In addition, concentration appears to fall with the size of a country's labor force and its level of development (Acemoglu and Zilibotti 1997). Poor, small, and mineral-abundant economies (or that depend on mining for foreign-exchange earnings) tend to have high levels of export concentration.

Regarding the determinants of terms-of-trade volatility, it is noteworthy that net exports of mining have not been affected after controlling for export concentration. Hence, mining exports appear to have only an indirect effect on terms-of-trade volatility via their effect on concentration. Similarly, net exports of natural resources seem to have no direct effect on GDP-per-capita volatility.

The econometric evidence suggests that the structural hypothesis is valid, but not necessarily the macroeconomic mismanagement hypothesis, even though the test for the former entails three equations, and the latter can be estimated in a single model. To the extent that this evidence can be interpreted as causal relationships, the main policy challenge for commodity-dependent economies seems to be related to industrial policies that may be able to stimulate export diversification, but not traditional industrial policies focused on specific sectors or products.

In contrast, the fiscal and monetary policy management required to ameliorate the transmission of external terms-of-trade volatility are better known. The evidence suggests that the curse does not systematically operate through this channel because the pass-through of external terms-of-trade volatility into GDP growth volatility does not rise with the level of net exports of natural resource or energy and mining products.

Notwithstanding the evidence discussed above, there may still be doubts about the direction of causality in the empirical analysis. Therefore, it is worthwhile to think more carefully about these issues, especially regarding the policy implications that could be derived from the potential effect of macroeconomic volatility on the structure of trade.

Table 7.2 Determinants of Export Concentration and GDP Growth Volatility, 1980–2005 (3SLS estimates)

Dependent variable	(1) Export concentration	(2) Terms-of-trade volatility	(3) GDP-per-capita growth volatility
Export concentration		0.351** (0.000)	
Net exports of energy and mining per worker	0.040** (0.000)	0.004 (0.170)	–0.003 (0.154)
Net exports of agriculture per worker	–0.036* (0.022)	–0.000 (0.941)	–0.002 (0.456)
Labor force (log, initial)	–0.058** (0.000)	0.015** (0.000)	–0.005** (0.000)
GDP per capita (log, initial)	–0.065** (0.000)		
Geographic trade over GDP	–0.002* (0.030)		
Terms-of-trade volatility			0.310** (0.000)
Observations	101	101	101
Pseudo R-squared	0.541	0.505	0.295
F-stat (p-value)	0.000	0.000	0.000
Adj. R-squared/First Stage	0.519	0.309	0.257

Source: Authors' calculations; see text.
Notes: ** and * represent statistically significant at the 1 and 5 percent levels. Cross-equation error correlations are assumed to be unstructured. All explanatory variables, except the dependent variables (export concentration, terms-of-trade volatility, and GDP-per-capita growth volatility) are assumed to be exogenous. Volatility is measured by the standard deviation of the annual growth rate of each variable during 1980–2005. The "first-stage" estimates are not reported. P-values appear inside parentheses and correspond to standard errors adjusted for degrees of freedom due to finite-sample assumptions. "Initial" means that the observation is from 1980; the results correspond to cross-sectional estimates for 1980–2005. Intercepts are not reported. GDP = gross domestic product; 3SLS = Three-Stage Least Squares.

Volatility as a Determinant of Export Structure and Financial Development

An extension of the neoclassical framework that also considers the composition of trade as an endogenous outcome allows for country characteristics, other than factor endowments, to affect the composition of trade. Lederman and Xu (2007), for example, provide evidence showing that the structure of the trade balance (that is, net exports by types of goods) is affected by institutional features, infrastructure, the level of innovation, and even macroeconomic volatility, even when natural resources and physical and human capital also play a role.

A long literature has studied the impact of exchange rate volatility and exchange rate regimes on trade flows (Clark et al. 2004). The initial motivation behind this literature was that in the absence of access to hedging mechanisms, risk-averse exporters would be adversely affected by currency risk and exports would be reduced (Clark 1973). However, this logic depends on a series of assumptions and has been challenged both theoretically and empirically. Overall, the current consensus seems to be that there is, at most, a weak negative effect of exchange rate volatility on aggregate trade flows.

To some extent, the literature's emphasis on the volume of trade has overlooked the impact of exchange rate volatility on the composition of trade. On the theoretical side, various models emphasize that exchange rate volatility may have differential effects across firms, depending on their ability to hedge the currency risk. For instance, Clark (1973) highlights the importance of the use of imported inputs as a natural hedge against fluctuations of the exchange rate. More recent papers also discuss the role of currency derivatives in reducing exposure to exchange rate risk (Wei 1999). Other recent papers, such as Caballero and Lorenzoni (2007), emphasize financial constraints as a determinant of a firm's ability to survive fluctuations in the exchange rate.

Empirically, Broda and Romalis (2003) and Clark et al. (2004) show that firms producing homogeneous goods tend to be relatively less affected by exchange rate volatility than firms producing differentiated products. The impact of exchange rate volatility on the structure of trade was explored by Raddatz (2011), a study commissioned as background for this book. Raddatz starts from the premise that exchange rate volatility affects relatively more firms and industries that are less able to hedge against exchange rate risk. It focuses on a specific aspect of industry heterogeneity that has not been directly addressed in the existing literature: the natural hedge against exchange rate fluctuations provided by the correlation of a good's price with a country's nominal exchange rate. That is, firms exporting goods whose international price commoves negatively with the home country's nominal exchange rate are naturally protected against exchange rate risk. Therefore, if this risk matters, they should be relatively less affected by exchange rate volatility. The possibility that this natural hedge offers some protection to firms is supported by evidence that firms whose income is positively correlated with the exchange rate, such as those in more tradable sectors, have a higher fraction of foreign currency–denominated liabilities (Bleakley and Cowan 2008). If this mechanism is empirically relevant, the structure of trade should endogenously shift toward industries producing goods that offer a natural hedge against exchange rate fluctuations in countries with high exchange rate volatility. Raddatz (2011) formally tested this hypothesis using data on the composition of exports of 106 countries across 752 commodities during 1984–2000. Raddatz also examined the correlation of these commodities' global unit values and each of these countries' nominal exchange rates. The idea that the price of some goods may be correlated with fluctuations in the nominal exchange rate has been present in a recent literature on "commodity currencies" (Cashin, Céspedes, and sahay 2004; Chen and Rogoff 2003). Commodity currencies fluctuate with the average price of the commodities exported by the country. Typical examples of commodity currencies are New Zealand and Australia. Because of this correlation, the price in local currency of these commodities and of any other sector whose price is correlated with them will be stable relative to other products.

The results from Raddatz (2011) indicate that the natural hedge against exchange rate volatility provided by a negative correlation between a commodity's international price and a country's nominal exchange rate matters for that country's export patterns. This proves to be the case even after controlling for other standard determinants of export composition, such as the factor endowments and the export patterns of countries with similar income levels.

The quantitative implication of the results in Raddatz (2011) is that a standard deviation increase in exchange rate volatility, corresponding to 60 percentage points, would lead to an increase of 10 percentage points in the within-country export share of a commodity at the 25th percentile of correlation relative to that of a commodity at the 75th percentile of correlation. This difference is about 15 percent of the typical difference in shares across commodities.

The mechanism is even stronger in explaining differences in the share of global exports of a given commodity captured by a country. In this case, a similar increase in volatility would result in a relative increase of two percentage points in favor of the sector with a strong negative correlation, which corresponds to 10 percent of the typical growth difference between sectors at the 25th and 75th percentiles of export growth shares. Moreover, these growth differences translate into large share differentials in steady state, resulting in an interquartile relative share increase of 40 percent. Similar results are obtained when comparing the role of natural hedging across exchange rate regimes instead of using an ex-post measure of exchange rate volatility.

A commodity's natural hedge is related to its importance in a country's commodity basket mainly under flexible exchange rate regimes. A series of robustness tests show that these results are not crucially driven by specific measures, countries, or commodities. Looking deeper into the drivers of the main result, additional evidence discussed in Raddatz (2011) suggests that a commodity's natural hedge has a discontinuous impact on its export share. A commodity whose price exhibits a small negative or positive correlation with a country's nominal exchange rate is only marginally favored or affected in terms of its weight on the country's exports basket. However, the relevance of a natural hedge increases more than proportionally for commodities with large correlations. Having a large negative or positive price correlation confers an important competitive advantage or disadvantage, respectively.

The results in Raddatz (2011) also show that the importance of a natural hedge against exchange rate fluctuations is inversely related to the availability of formal hedging instruments. Perhaps more important, a well-developed market for foreign exchange rate derivatives associated with a given country's currency weakens the relation between a commodity price's correlation with the country's exchange rate and its importance on the country's export basket in high exchange rate volatility environments. Broader measures of the development of financial markets do not seem to have such an effect on the importance of a natural hedge for export composition, suggesting that the relevant dimension of financial development for this mechanism is the widespread availability of exchange rate derivatives.

From a policy perspective, the findings by Raddatz (2011) emphasize the endogeneity of the composition of exports, and show that it is affected by factors beyond the standard relative factor abundance postulated by neoclassical trade theory. These factors are also related to the ability of the firm to cope with the risks associated with exporting goods. If in fact what an economy exports matters, as conjectured by Hausmann et al (2007), addressing some of these financial market imperfections may be a better way to move toward a first-best export composition than engaging in industrial policy. In particular, the development of exchange rate derivatives plays an important role in weakening the relation between a sector's natural hedge and export composition. Nonetheless, in the spirit of giving industrial policy a chance, the focus will turn next to the possibility of a flawless industrial policy succeeding in picking winning export products.

The Distribution of Manufactured Exports

Easterly, Reshef, and Schwenkenberg (2009) demonstrate that manufacturing export success shows a remarkable degree of specialization for virtually all countries. Manufacturing exports in each country are dominated by a few "big hits," which account for most of the export value, and where the "hit" includes finding both the right product and the right market.

The specificity and description of the "hits" are far from intuitive. Out of 2,985 possible products and 217 possible destinations, the Arab

Republic of Egypt derives 23 percent of its total manufacturing exports from exporting one product—"Ceramic bathroom kitchen sanitary items not porcelain"—to one destination, Italy, capturing 94 percent of the Italian import market for that product. Fiji sends "Women's, girl's suits, of cotton, not knit" to the United States (14 percent of Fiji manufacturing exports, 42 percent of U.S. imports of that product). The Philippines derives 10 percent of their manufacturing exports from sending "Electronic integrated circuits/micro-assemblies, [not elsewhere specified]" to the U.S. (80 percent of U.S. imports of that product). Nigeria earns 10 percent of its manufacturing exports from shipping "Floating docks, special function vessels not elsewhere specified" to Norway, constituting 84 percent of Norwegian imports of that product.

Examining the top pairs of what would seem to be fairly similar countries reveals a surprising diversity of products and destinations. Why does Colombia export paint pigment to the United States, Costa Rica export data processing equipment, and Peru, T-shirts? Why does Guatemala export candles to the United States, and El Salvador, bath toilet and kitchen linens? Why does Honduras export soap to El Salvador, while Nicaragua exports bathroom porcelain to Costa Rica? Why does Côte d'Ivoire export perfume to Ghana, while Ghana exports plastic tables and kitchenware to Togo? Why does Uganda export electro-diagnostic apparatuses to India, while Malawi exports small motorcycle engines to Japan? The remarkable specialization across products and destinations emerges in high concentration ratios. The top 1 percent of product destination pairs accounts for an average of 52 percent of manufacturing export value for 151 countries.

The difference between successful and unsuccessful exporters is found not in the degree of specialization, but in the scale of the "big hits." For example, a significant part of the Republic of Korea's superior performance relative to Tanzania as a manufacturing exporter is exemplified by Korea earning $13 billion from its top three manufacturing exports, while Tanzania earned only $4 million from its top three exports. The bad news is that the probability of finding a big hit ex ante decreases exponentially with the magnitude of the hit. Easterly and coauthors (2009) demonstrate that the upper part of the distribution of export values across products (defined both by destination and by 6-digit industry classifications) is close to following a power law. In other words, it is very difficult to predict big hits.

The fact that manufactured exports tend to be highly concentrated everywhere points to the conclusion that choosing products to subsidize might not result in greater export diversification. The factors of production necessary to produce and export the next big hit need to come from somewhere, and it is likely that the expansion of one activity must be accompanied by the decline of another.

Suppose that without government failures old-style industrial policy succeeds in preselecting the big hits. Given the strong, stylized facts discussed above, would this policy also succeed in diversifying the export portfolio of a small, underdeveloped economy with abundant natural resources? There is no existing evidence or theoretical framework that could explain how the emergence of one big hit affects other existing exports and the prices of their required factors of production.

The following chapter returns to the policy challenges and trade-offs that perhaps should be kept in mind in the pursuit of pro-diversification policies.

Notes

1. Cadot, Carrere, and Strauss-Kahn (2011) later confirmed the findings in Klinger and Lederman (2004, 2006) regarding the U-shape relationship between export concentration and GDP per capita. They asked, "What's behind the hump?" which is of import mainly for high-income countries.

2. The additional results are available from the authors upon request.

8

Conclusion and Policy Reflections

Does what a country exports matter? The answer can be broken down into several parts, although the bottom line is that "*how* you export matters more."

First, what a country exports probably does matter. Externalities and rents exist, and there is no reason to believe that they are associated with all goods equally. In the former case, there is clearly an argument for interventions to encourage such goods more than the market would naturally do.

Second, the literature still offers us no confident policy guidance on what those goods might be. Measurement of externalities is notoriously difficult, and this study has argued that the shortcuts offered to get around this measurement issue—showing that goods thought a priori to have externalities that positively affect growth—have proven weak pillars for policy makers to rely on. The advice to stay out of natural resource industries and to get into high-tech industries, those which rich countries already produce, or those offering potential to enter new industries, either does not prove robust empirically or, where no empirical test is offered, raises substantial conceptual concerns. Perhaps the market is missing good opportunities, but it is not apparent at this point that government (or we) can see them any more clearly.

Third, the policy debate needs to focus far more on the vast heterogeneity of experiences within any given sector. Although the study has shown that there is no robust evidence of a resource curse, there definitely are countries that appear to have suffered as a result of having resources, just as there are tremendous success stories, including much of the industrialized world today. The production technologies used to produce a good, and the "knowledge intensity" of that process, can vary greatly across countries. The returns to skilled labor vary as much across countries as across goods. The range of quality within much disaggregated categories of goods is so large that some have argued that understanding the allocation of quality across countries is more germane than that of goods. Finally, in a very fragmented global production system, identical goods on the export registers can mask different stages of the production process undertaken in each country. Some countries invent cutting-edge computers, some merely assemble them. These are distinct tasks with, in all likelihood, a different potential for externalities and rents. The focus on goods in the Industrial Policy literature is, itself, a very crude and misleading shortcut, compounded by the fact that global data on tasks are virtually nonexistent.

The lack of robust empirical indicators to help select products for special treatment and the overwhelming evidence of heterogeneity within goods should shift the debate to understanding how countries can produce whatever it is they produce in ways that more effectively drive economic development. More generally, the process of moving toward frontier productivity, quality, or tasks can be viewed through the standard convergence puzzle: Why, given the global stock of know-how, do developing countries not catch up more rapidly? This leads almost immediately back to the underlying factor endowments of a country very broadly construed. Asking why some countries produce only low-quality wine is similar to asking about the quality of winemakers, their use of modern technologies, and the availability of suitable infrastructure in that country, including the *terroire* (the quality of the land and climate). Asking why one country produces 10 times more patents per exported computer than another is a question about the quality of the scientific human capital and the functioning of the national innovation system.

Fourth, diversification, to a point, does appear important for reducing the negative externality posed by terms-of-trade volatility. Small, poor, and natural resource–dependent economies do tend to have more concentrated export baskets than large, rich countries that are net importers of mining products. However, here again, the extraordinary concentration of exports in a few product-destination pairs suggests that picking a basket of goods with particular covariances among them is also likely to be difficult. Providing a fertile business environment where new industries can establish roots is likely to be the best bet. Furthermore, to the extent that natural resource–abundant countries face higher external volatility due to terms-of-trade volatility driven by export concentration, then the standard recipe of prudent macroeconomic management policies might suffice. However, it is also noteworthy that such countries do not exhibit, on average, a higher tendency to pass on the external volatility into domestic growth volatility than net importers of natural resources.

Finally, one must be careful even with infallible industrial policies that pick the next big hit because successful policies might result in the emergence of a dynamic export industry that could rise at the expense of others that utilize similar factors of production. Thus, industrial policy is not the obvious first-best policy choice, even in a world without government failures. Policies to promote financial development, establish fiscal rules, and promote exports more broadly rather than specific products or industries are probably a superior choice for governments.

The above conclusions imply an important role for government, even if it does not involve picking goods or tasks. Market failures abound in the provision of infrastructure, the accumulation of human capital, the establishment of trade networks, and the creation and management of ideas. Appropriation externalities in the discovery process and in the adaptation of new processes and technologies to existing industries are well documented. All these suggest "horizontalish" policies that seek to raise the overall ability of a country to increase productivity and quality, or to move to more sophisticated tasks. This term is used because, even though no attempt is made to target sectors, industries benefit differentially from the general provision of any factor. Resolving coordination failures within existing industries also requires government intervention. In sum, what can be more confidently argued is that *how* a country exports is central. This notion, rather than what a country exports, should be the focus of policy makers.

Bibliography

Acemoglu, D. and F. Zilibotti. 1997. "Was Prometheus Unbound by Chance? Risk, Diversification and Growth." *Journal of Political Economy* 105(4): 709–751. University of Chicago Press.

Acemoglu, Daron, Pol Antras and Elhanan Helpman. 2007. "Contracts and Technology Adoption." *The American Economic Review* 97(3): 916–943.

Acemoglu, Daron, and James Robinson. 2005. "Unbundling Institutions." *Journal of Political Economy* 113(5): 949–95.

Acemoglu, Daron, Simon Johnson, and James Robinson. 2002. "Reversal of Fortune: Geography and Institutions in the Making of the Modern World Income Distribution." *Quarterly Journal of Economics* 117(4): 1231–294.

———. 2001. "The Colonial Origins of Comparative Development: An Empirical Investigation." *American Economic Review* 91(5): 1369–401.

Alesina, Alberto, and Allan Drazen. 1991. "Why Are Stabilizations Delayed?" *American Economic Review* 81(5): 1170–188.

Alexeev, Michael, and Robert Conrad. 2009. "The Elusive Curse of Oil." *Review of Economics and Statistics.* 91(3): 586–98.

Alvarez, Roberto, and Rodrigo Fuentes. 2009. "The Quality of Trade: Unit Value Dynamics." Unpublished work. Central Bank of Chile and Department of Economics, Catholic University of Chile, Santiago, Chile.

Antràs, Pol, Luis Garicano, and Esteban Rossi-Hansberg. 2006. "Organizing Off-shoring: Middle Managers and Communication Costs," in Helpman, E., D. Marin, and T. Verdier, editors. *The Organization of Firms in a Global Economy.* Harvard University Press, pp. 311–339.

Antweiler, Werner, and Daniel Trefler. 2002. "Increasing Returns and All That: A View from Trade." *American Economic Review* 92(1): 93–119.

Artuc, Erhan, Shubham Chaudhuri and John McLaren. 2010. "Trade Shocks and Labor Adjustment: A Structural Empirical Approach." *American Economic Review* 100(3): 1008–1045.

Auty, Richard M. 2006. "Patterns of Rent-Extraction and Deployment in Developing Countries: Implications for Governance, Economic Policy, and Performance." *WIDER Research Paper* 2006/16. Helsinki: United Nations University, World Institute for Development Economics Research.

Auty, Richard M., ed. 2001a. Resource Abundance and Economic Development. Oxford University Press.

Auty, Richard M. 2001b. "The Political Economy of Resource-Driven Growth." *European Economic Review* 45(4–6): 839–46.

———. 2000. "How Natural Resources Affect Economic Development." *Development Policy Review* 18(4): 347–64.

———. 1993. Sustaining Development in Mineral Economies: The Resource Curse Thesis. London and New York: Routledge.

Baldwin, R. 1989a. "Exporting the capital markets: Comparative advantage and capital market imperfection, in D Audretsch, L Sleuwaegen and H. Yamawaki eds. The Convergence of International and Domestic Markets, North-Holland, New York.

―――. 1989b. "Exporting the capital markets: Comparative advantage and capital market imperfection," in D. Audretsch, L Sleuwaegen and H. Yamawaki, editors, *The Convergence of International and Domestic Markets.* North-Holland: New York.

―――. 1969. "The Case against Infant Industry Protection." *Journal of Political Economy* 77:295–305 (May/June).

Baldwin, Richard and Frédéric Robert-Nicoud. 2010. "Trade-in-goods and trade-in-tasks: An Integrating Framework." Graduate Institute, Geneva; University of Geneva. March.

Bardan, P and K. Kletzer. 1987. "Credit markets and patterns of International Trade." *Journal of Development Economics* 27:57–70.

Barro, Robert J., and Jong-Wha Lee. 2000. "International Data on Educational Attainment: Updates and Implications." *National Bureau of Economic Research Working Paper* 7911. Cambridge, Mass.: National Bureau of Economic Research.

Barro, Robert. 1991. "Economic Growth in a Cross-Section of Countries." *Quarterly Journal of Economics* 106(2): 407–43.

Bastos, P and J. Silva. 2008. "The Quality of a Firm's Exports: Where you Export to Matters" *University of Nottingham Research Paper Series* 2008:18.

Basu, S., and J. Fernald. 2007. Information and Communications Technology as a General-Purpose Technology: Evidence from U.S Industry Data, *German Economic Review.*

Basu, Susanto, and John G. Fernald. 1995. "Are Apparent Productive Spillovers a Figment Of Specification Error?" *Journal of Monetary Economics* 36: 165–88.

Beck, Thorsten. 2002. "Financial development and international trade: Is there a link?" *Journal of International Economics* Elsevier, vol. 57(1): 107–131.

Beck, Thorsten, Asli Demirgüç-Kunt and Ross Levine. 2000. "A New Database on Financial Development and Structure," *World Bank Economic Review* 14: 597–605.

Besedes, Tibor and Prusa, Thomas J. 2006. "Product differentiation and duration of US import trade," *Journal of International Economics* Elsevier, vol. 70(2): 339–358, December.

Bhagwati, J. 1968. The Theory and Practice of Commercial Policy: Departures from Unified Exchange Rates. Special Papers in International Economics. New Jersey: Princeton University Press.

Bleakley, H. and K. Cowan. 2008. "Corporate Dollar Debt and Depreciations: Much Ado About Nothing?" *Review of Economics and Statistics* 90 (4): 612–626.

Blomström, Magnus, and Ari Kokko. 2007. "From Natural Resources to High-Tech Production: The Evolution of Industrial Competitivness in Sweden and Finland." In Natural Resources: Neither Curse nor Destiny, edited by Daniel Lederman and William F. Maloney, chapter 8. Stanford University Press.

Blomström, Magnus, and Patricio Meller. 1991. Diverging Paths: Comparing a Century of Scandinavian and Latin American Economic Development. Washington D.C.: Inter-American Development Bank.

Brambilla, Irene, Daniel Lederman and Guido Porto. 2012. "Exports, Export Destinations and Skills." *American Economic Review*, forthcoming. Draft version published as *National Bureau for Economic Research Working Paper* 15995, Cambridge, Massachusetts.

Brambilla, Irene, Rafael Dix-Carneiro, Daniel Lederman, and Guido Porto. 2011. "Exports, Skills and the Wages of Seven Million Latin American Workers." *The World Bank Economic Review*. Draft version published as "Exports, Skills and the Wages of Five Million Latin American Workers." *World Bank Policy Research Working Paper* 5246. World Bank, Washington, DC.

Bravo-Ortega, Claudio, and José de Gregorio. 2007. "The Relative Richness of the Poor: Natural Resources, Human Capital, and Economic Growth." In Natural Resources: Neither Curse nor Destiny, edited by Daniel Lederman and William F. Maloney, chapter 6. Stanford University Press.

Breznitz, Dan and Michael Murphree. 2011. *The Run of the Red Queen* Yale University Press.

Bravo-Ortega, Claudio, and José de Gregorio. 2007. "The Relative Richness of the Poor? Natural Resources, Human Capital, and Economic Growth." In Natural Resources: Neither Curse nor Destiny, edited by Daniel Lederman and William F. Maloney, chapter 4. Stanford University Press.

Broda, C., and J. Romalis. 2003. "Identifying the Relationship between Trade and Exchange Rate Volatility." Technical Report, Chicago Graduate School of Business, Chicago, IL

Brooks, E. 2006. Why don't firms export more? Product Quality and Colombian Plants" *Journal of Development Economics* 80:160–178.

Brunnschweiler, Christina N. 2008. "Cursing the Blessings? Natural Resource Abundance, Institutions, and Economic Growth." *World Development* 36(3): 399–419.

Bustos, Paula. 2010. "Trade Liberalization, Exports and Technology Upgrading: Evidence on the Impact of MERCOSUR on Argentinean Firms." *American Economic Review*, forthcoming.

Caballero, R.J. and G. Lorenzoni. 2007. "Persistent Appreciations and Overshooting: A Normative Analysis." Technical Report, National Bureau for Economic Research Working Paper 2007, Cambridge, MA.

Cadot, Olivier, Celine Carrere, and Vanessa Strauss-Kahn. 2011. "Export Diversification: What's Behind the Hump?" *The Review of Economics and Statistics* 93(2): 590–605.

Card, David. 1999. "The Causal Effect of Education on Earnings," in Ashenfelter Orley and David Card, editors, *Handbook of Labor Economics,* Vol. 3: 1801–1863. Elsevier Science B.V.

Cashin, P., L.F. Céspedes, and R. Sahay, 2004. "Commodity Currencies and the Real Exchange Rate." *Journal of Development Economics* 75 (1): 239–268.

Chen, Y. and K. Rogoff. 2003. "Commodity Currencies." *Journal of International Economics* 60 (1): 133–160.

Ciccone, Antonio, and Giovanni Peri. 2006. "Identifying Human Capital Externalities: Theory with Applications." *Review of Economic Studies* 73: 381–412.

Ciccone, Antonio, and Marek Jarocinski. 2010. "Determinants of Economic Growth: Will Data Tell?" *American Economic Journal* Macroeconomics, forthcoming.

Ciccone, Antonio, Federico Cingano, and Piero Cipollone. 2004. "The Private and Social Return to Schooling in Italy." *Giornale degli Economisti e Annali di Economia* 63(3-4): 413–444. December.

Clark, P., N. Tamirisa, S.J. Wei, A. Sadikov, and L. Zeng. 2004. "Exchange rate volatility and trade flows-some new evidence." Technical Report,Washington, DC: International Monetary Fund.

Clark, P.B. 1973. "Uncertainty, Exchange Rate Risk, and the Level of International Trade." *Economic Inquiry* 11 (3): 302–313.

Corden, W. Max, and J. Peter Neary. 1982. "Booming Sector and De-Industrialization in a Small Open Economy." *The Economic Journal* 92(368): 825–48.

Cuddington, John T., Rodney Ludema, and Shamila A. Jayasuriya. 2007. "Prebisch-Singer Redux." In: *Natural Resources: Neither Curse nor Destiny*, edited by Daniel Lederman and William F. Maloney, chapter 5. Stanford University Press.

Czelusta, Jesse W. 2001. "Natural Resources, Economic Growth, and Technical Change: Lessons from Australia and the United States." Stanford University.

Davis, Graham. 1995. "Learning to Love the Dutch Disease: Evidence from the Mineral Economies." *World Development* 23(10): 1765–79.

De Long, Bradford, and Lawrence Summers. 1992. "Equipment Investment and Economic Growth." *Quarterly Journal of Economics* 106(2): 455–502.

Do, Q. and A. Levchenko. 2007. "Comparative Advantage, Demand for external Finance, and Financial Development." *Journal of Financial Economics* 86: 796–834.

Dollar, David, and Aart Kraay. 2003. "Institutions, Trade, and Growth." *Journal of Monetary Economics* 50(1): 133–62.

Dunning, Thad. 2008a. Crude Democracy: Natural Resource Wealth and Political Regimes. Cambridge Studies in Comparative Politics. Cambridge University Press.

———. 2008b. "Model Specification in Instrumental-Variables Regression." *Political Analysis* 16(3): 290–302.

Dunning, Thad. 2005. "Resource Dependence, Economic Performance, and Political Stability." *Journal of Conflict Resolution* 49(4): 451–82.

Durlauf, Steven N., Andros Kourtellos, and Artur Minkin. 2001. "The Local Solow Growth Model." *European Economic Review* 45(4–6): 928–40.

Easterly, W., A. Reshef, and J. Schwenkenberg. 2009. "The Power of Exports." *World Bank Policy Research Working Paper* 5081. World Bank, Washington, DC.

Easterly, William, and Ross Levine. 2002 "Tropics, Germs, and Crops: How Endowments Influence Economic Development." University of Minnesota.

Eaton, Jonathan, Marcela Eslava, Maurice Kugler, and James Tybout. 2007. "Export Dynamics in Colombia: Firm-Level Evidence." *NBER Working Paper* 13351, National Bureau of Economic Research, Inc., Cambridge, MA.

Estevadeordal, Antoni, and Alan M. Taylor. 2002. "A Century of Missing Trade?" *American Economic Review* 92(1): 383–93.

Feenstra, Robert C. "US Imports, 1972-1994: Data and Concordances." *NBER Working Paper Series*. Working Paper 5515. Cambridge, MA. 1996.

Fernandes, A. M and C. Paunov. 2009. "Does Tougher Import Competition foster Product Quality Upgrading? PRWP 4894, World Bank, Washington, DC.

Findlay, Ronald, and Mats Lundahl. 1994. "Natural Resources, 'Vent-for-Surplus,' and the Staples Theory." In From Classical Economics to Development Economics, edited by Gerald M Meir. New York: St. Martin's Press.

Frankel, Jeffrey A., and David Romer. 1999. "Does Trade Cause Growth?" American Economic Review 89(3): 379–99.

Fujita, Masahisa, Paul Krugman, and Anthony J. Venables. 1999. The Spatial Economy: Cities, Regions, and International Trade. MIT Press.

Ganslandt, M and J.R. Markusen. 2000. Standards and related regulations in international trade: A modeling approach. Quantifying the impact of technical barriers to trade: Can it be done? Studies in International Economics, Ann Arbor: University of Michigan Press.

Gelb, Alan. 1988. Oil Windfalls: Blessing or Curse? Oxford University Press.

Glaeser, Edward L., and others. 2004. "Do Institutions Cause Growth?" Journal of Economic Growth 9(3): 271–303.

Goh, Keng Swee. 1972. The Economics of Modernization and Other Essays. Singapore: Asia Pacific Press. Cited in Alwyn Young, "A Tale of Two Cities: Factor Accumulation and Technical Change in Hong Kong and Singapore," 1996 NBER Macroeconomics Annual. Cambridge, MA: MIT Press, pp. 13–54.

Goldstein, M and M. S. Khan. 1985. "Income and Price Effects in Foreign Trade" in R. W. Jones and P.B. Kenen, eds. Handbook of International Economics. Volume II, chapter 20.

Greenwood, Jeremy and Boyan Jovanovic. 1990. "Financial Development, Growth, and Distribution of Income." Journal of Political Economy 98(5): 1076–1107.

Griliches, Zvi. 1977. "Estimating the Returns to Schooling: Some Econometric Problems." Econometrica 45: 1–22.

Grossman G. and A. Razin. 1985. Direct Foreing Investment and Choice of Technique under Uncertainty" Oxford Economic Papers 37:4 606–620.

Grossman, G. M. and E. Rossi-Hansberg. 2008. "Trading Tasks: A Simple Theory of Offshoring," American Economic Review, 98:5, 1978–1997

———. 2006. "The Rise of Offshoring: It's Not Wine for Cloth Anymore." In The New Economic Geography: Effects and Policy Implications, Jackson Hole Conference Volume, Federal Reserve Bank of Kansas City

Gylfason, Thorvaldur, Tryggvi Thor Herbertsson, and Gylfi Zoega. 1999. "A Mixed Blessing: Natural Resources and Economic Growth." Macroeconomic Dynamics 3(2): 204–25.

Gylfason, Thorvaldur. 2001. "Natural Resources, Education, and Economic Development." European Economic Review 45(4–6): 847–59.

Hallak, J.C., and P. Schott 2008, "Estimating Cross Country Differences in Product Quality." NBER Working Paper Number 13807. Cambridge, MA.

Hallak, J.C. and J. Sivadasan. 2007. Productivity, Quality and Exporting Behavior Under Minimum Quality Requirements.

Harrison, A. and A. Rodriguez-Clare. 2010. "Trade, Foreign Investment, and Industrial Policy for Developing Countries." Chapter 63 in Handbook of Development Economics, edited by D. Rodrik and M. Rosenzweig. North-Holland: New York.

Hausmann, R and C. A. Hidalgo. 2010. Country diversification, product ubiquity, and economic divergence.

———. 2009. The Building Blocks of Economic Complexity. *Proceedings of the National Academy of Sciences* 106(26):10,570–10,575.

Hausmann, R, Hwang, J, and D. Rodrik. 2007. "What You Export Matters." *Journal of Economic Growth*. 12:1–25.

Hausmann, Ricardo and Bailey Klinger, 2006. "South Africa's Export Predicament." Center for International Development, *Harvard University Working Paper* 129, Cambridge, MA.

Hausmann R., and B. Klinger. 2007. "The Structure of the Product Space and the Evolution of Comparative Advantage." Center for International Development, *Harvard University Working Paper* 146, Cambridge, MA.

———. 2006. "Structural Transformation and Patterns of Comparative Advantage in the Product Space" Center for International Development, *Harvard University Working Paper* No. 128, Cambridge, MA.

Hausmann, R. and D. Rodrik. 2003a. "Economic development as self-discovery." *Journal of Development Economics* 72: 603–633.

Hausmann, Ricardo, and Francisco Rodríguez, eds. Forthcoming. Venezuela: Anatomy of a Collapse. Harvard University, Kennedy School of Government.

Hidalgo, C. 2010. "The Dynamics of Economic Complexity and the Product Space over a 42-Year Period." *CID Working Paper* 189.

Hidalgo, C.A., B. Klinger, A.L. Barabasi, and R. Hausmann. 2007. "The Product Space Conditions the Development of Nations." *Science* 371: 482–487.

Hummels, D and P. J. Klenow. 2005. "The Variety and Quality of a Nation's Exports" *American Economic Review* 95(3):704–723.

Humphreys, Macartan, Jeffrey D. Sachs, and Joseph E. Stiglitz, eds. 2007. Escaping the Resource Curse. Columbia University Press.

Hwang, J. 2006. "Introduction of New Goods, Convergence and Growth," Unpublished work. Harvard University

Iacovone, L. and B. Jovorcik. 2008. Shipping Good Tequila Out: Investment, domestic Unit Values and Entry of Multi-0Product Plants into Export Markets," University of Oxford. Unpublished work.

Imbs, J. and Wacziarg, R. 2003. "Stages of diversification." *The American Economic Review* 93(1): 63–86.

Innis, Harold. 1933. Problems of Staple Production in Canada. University of Toronto Press.

Irwin, Douglas A. 2000. "How Did the United States Become a Net Exporter of Manufactured Goods?" *Working Paper* 7638. Cambridge, Mass.: National Bureau of Economic Research.

Isham, Jonathan, and others. 2005. "The Varieties of Resource Experience: Natural Resource Export Structures and the Political Economy of Economic Growth." *World Bank Economic Review* 19(2): 141–74. World Bank, Washington, DC.

Karl, Terry Lynn. 1997. The Paradox of Plenty: Oil Booms and Petro-States. University of California Press.

Kee, H.L., A. Nicita, and M. Olarreaga. 2009. "Estimating Trade Restrictiveness Indices." *Economic Journal* 119: 172–99.

———. 2008a. "Import Demand Elasticities and Trade Distortions." *Review of Economics and Statistics* 90(4): 666–682.

Khandelwal, A. 2008. "The Long and Short (of) Quality Ladders." Columbia Business School. Unpublished work.

Klinger, Bailey, and Daniel Lederman. 2011. "Export Discoveries, Diversification and Barriers to Entry." *Economic Systems* 35: 64–83.

Klinger, Bailey, and Daniel Lederman. 2006. "Diversification, Innovation, and Imitation inside the Global Technological Frontier." *World Bank Policy Research Working Paper* 3872. World Bank, Washington, DC.

———. 2004. "Discovery and Development: An Empirical Exploration of 'New' Products." *World Bank Policy Research Working Paper* 3450. World Bank, Washington, DC.

Kobrin, S. J. 2007. "Multinational Firms, Economic Development, and the Emergence of 'Trade in Tasks.' The Wharton School, University of Pennsylvania. Unpublished work.

Koopmans, Robert, Zhi Wang, and Shang-Jin Wei. 2008. "How Much of Chinese Exports is Really Made in China? Assessing Domestic Value-Added When Processing Trade is Pervasive." *NBER Working Paper* 14109. Cambridge, MA.

Kraemer, Kenneth L., Greg Linden, and Jason Dedrick. 2011. "Capturing Value in Global Networks: Apple's iPad and iPhone." Unpublished work. University of California, Irvine, University of California, Berkeley, and Syracuse University. http://pcic.merage.uci.edu/papers/2011/Value_iPad_iPhone.pdf

Krishna, Pravin, and William F. Maloney 2011 "Export Unit Value Dynamics: Some Stylized Facts" World Bank Policy Research Working Paper. 5701

———. 2010 "Growth and Risk: A View from International Trade" Unpublished work. Washington, DC: World Bank

Krueger, Alan B, and Mikael Lindahl. 2001. "Education: For What and For Whom?" *Journal of Economic Literature* 39(4): 1101–1136.

Krueger, Anne O. 1974. "The Political Economy of the Rent-Seeking Society." *American Economic Review* 64(3): 291–303.

Krueger, Alan B., and Lawrence H. Summers. 1988. "Efficiency Wages and Inter-Industry Wage Structure." *Econometrica* 56(2) 259–93.

Kugler, M., and E. Verhoogen. 2008. "The Quality-Complementarity Hypothesis: Theory and Evidence from Colombia," *NBER Working Papers* 14418, National Bureau of Economic Research, Inc.

Lall, Sanjaya and John Weiss, and Jinkang Zhang. 2006. "The 'Sophistication'of Exports: A New Trade Measure" *World Development* Vol. 34 (2): 222–237.

Larsen, Røed E. 2004. "Escaping the Resources and the Dutch Disease? When and Why Norway Caught up with and Forged ahead of Its Neighbours." Discussion Paper 377. Statistics Norway Research Department.

Leamer, Edward E. 1984. *Sources of Comparative Advantage: Theory and Evidence.* Cambridge MA: MIT Press.

Leamer, Edward E. 1995. "The Heckscher-Ohlin Model in Theory and Practice." Princeton Studies in International Finance 77. Princeton University.

Lederman, Daniel. 2010. "A Multi-Level International Analysis of Product Innovation." *Journal of International Business Studies* 41(4): 606–619.

Lederman, Daniel and L. Colin Xu. 2007. "Comparative Advantage and Trade Intensity: Are Traditional Endowments Destiny?" In: *Natural Resources: Neither Curse nor Destiny,* edited by Daniel Lederman and William F. Maloney, chapter 10. Stanford University Press.

Lederman, Daniel, and William F. Maloney. 2008. "In Search of the Missing Resource Curse." *Economía, Journal of the Latin American and Caribbean Economic Association* 9(1): 1–57.

Lederman, Daniel, and William F. Maloney, eds. 2007a. Natural Resources: Neither Curse nor Destiny. Stanford University Press.

Lederman, Daniel, and William F. Maloney. 2007b. "Trade Structure and Growth." In: *Natural Resources: Neither Curse nor Destiny*. Stanford University Press.

———. 2007c. "Trade Structure and Growth." Chapter 2 in *Natural Resources, Neither Curse nor Destiny*, edited by D. Lederman and W. Maloney. Washington, DC: World Bank and Stanford University Press.

———. 2006. "Innovation in Mexico: NAFTA Is Not Enough." Chapter 13 in *Global Integration and Technology Transfer*, edited by B. Hoekman and B. Smarzynska Javorcik. World Bank, Washington, DC and Palgrave Macmillan.

Lederman, Daniel, Andrés Rodríguez-Clare, and Daniel Xu. 2011. "Entrepreneurship and the Extensive Margin in Export Growth: A Microeconomic Accounting of Costa Rica's Export Growth, 1997–2007." *The World Bank Economic Review* 25(3): 543–61.

Lee, Donghoon, and Kenneth I. Wolpin. 2006. "Intersectoral Labor Mobility and the Growth of the Service Sector." *Econometrica* 74(1): 1–46.

Levchenko, A. A. 2007. Institutional quality and international Trade Review of Economic Studies 74:791–819.

Levine, Ross, and David Renelt. 1992. "A Sensitivity Analysis of Cross-Country Growth Regressions." *American Economic Review* 82(4): 942–63.

Linden, Greg, Kenneth L. Kraemer, and Jason Dedrick. 2009. "Who Captures Value in a Global Innovation Network? The Case of Apple's iPod." *Communications of the ACM* 52(3): 140–144.

Maddison, Angus. 1994. "Explaining the Economic Performance of Nations, 1820–1989." In Convergence of Productivity, edited by William J. Baumol, Richard R. Nelson, and Edward N. Wolff. Oxford University Press.

Maloney, William F. 2007. "Missed Opportunities: Innovation and Resource-Based Growth in Latin America." In Natural Resources: Neither Curse nor Destiny, edited by Daniel Lederman and William F. Maloney. Stanford University Press.

Mankiw, Gregory, David Romer, and David Weil. 1992. "A Contribution to the Empirics of Economic Growth." *Quarterly Journal of Economics* 107(2): 407–37.

Manzano, Osmel, and Roberto Rigobon. 2007. "Resource Curse or Debt Overhang?" In Natural Resources: Neither Curse nor Destiny, edited by Daniel Lederman and William F. Maloney. Stanford University Press.

Marshall, Monty G., and Keith Jaggers. 2002. "Polity IV Project: Political Regime Characteristics and Transitions, 1800–2002." University of Maryland, College Park, Center for International Development and Conflict Management.

Martin, Will, and Devashish Mitra. 2001. "Productivity Growth and Convergence in Agriculture and Manufacturing." *Economic Development and Cultural Change* 49(2): 403–22.

Mayer, W. 1984. "The infant-export industry argument." 17(2): 249–269.

McEvedy, Colin, and Richard Jones. 1978. Atlas of World Population History. New York: Facts on File.

Mehlum, Halvor, Karl Moene, and Ragnar Torvik. 2006. "Institutions and the Resource Curse." *Economic Journal* 116(508): 1–20.

Moreno, María Antonio, and Cameron A. Shelton. forthcoming. "Sleeping in the Bed One Makes: The Venezuelan Fiscal Policy Response to the Oil Boom." In

Venezuela: Anatomy of a Collapse, edited by Ricardo Hausmann and Francisco Rodríguez.

Mukerji, Purba, and Arvind Panagariya. 2009. "Within- and Across-Product Specialization Revisited." Unpublished work. Columbia University, New York.

Murshed, S. Mansoob. 2004. "When Does Natural Resource Abundance Lead to a Resource Curse?" Environmental Economics Programme Discussion Paper 04–11. The Hague: International Institute for Environment and Development.

Neary, J. Peter. 2003. "Competitive versus comparative advantage." *The World Economy* 26(4): 457–470.

Neumayer, Eric. 2004. "Does the 'Resource Curse' Hold for Growth in Genuine Income as Well?" *World Development* 32(10): 1627–640.

North, Douglas. 1955. "Location Theory and Regional Economic Growth." *Journal of Political Economy* 63: 243–58.

Nunn, Nathan. 2008. "The Long-Term Effects of Africa's Slave Trades." *Quarterly Journal of Economics* 123(1): 139–76.

Obstfeld, M. 1994. Risk Taking, global diversification and Growth. *The American Economic Review*, vol 84:(5)1310–1329.

Pack, H and K. Saggi. 2006. "The case for industrial policy: a critical survey." Unpublished work. Wharton School.

Panagariya, A., S. Shah and D. Mishra. 2001. "Demand Elasticities in International Trade: Are They Really Low?" *Journal of Development Economics* 64: 313–342.

———. 1996. "Demand Elasticities in International Trade- Are they Really Low" *World Bank Policy Research Working* Paper 1712. World Bank, Washington, DC.

Peretto, Pietro F. 2008. "Is the 'Curse of Natural Resources' Really a Curse?" *Economic Research Initiatives at Duke (ERID) Working Paper* 14. Duke University, Department of Economics.

Pavcnik, N., A. Blom, P. Goldberg, and N. Schady 2004. "Trade Liberalization and Industry Wage Structure: Evidence from Brazil." *World Bank Economic Review* 18(3): 319–44.

Pol Antràs, Luis Garicano and Esteban Rossi-Hansberg. 2006. Offshoring in a Knowledge Economy. *Quarterly Journal of Economics* 121(1):31–77

Prebisch, Raúl. 1962. "The Economic Development of Latin America and Its Principal Problems." Reprinted in *Economic Bulletin for Latin America* 7(1): 1–22.

Prebisch, Raúl. 1959. "Commercial Policy in the Underdeveloped Countries." *American Economic Review* 49: 251–273

Raddatz, Claudio. 2011. "Over the Hedge: Exchange Rate Volatility, Commodity Price Correlations, and the Structure of Trade." *Policy Research Working Paper* 5590, World Bank, Washington, DC.

Rajan, Raghuram, and Luigi Zingales. 2003. Saving Capitalism from the Capitalists: Unleashing the Power of Financial Markets to Create Wealth and Spread Opportunity. New York: Crown Business.

Rodríguez, Francisco, and Adam J. Gomolin. Forthcoming. "Anarchy, State, and Dystopia: Venezuelan Economic Institutions before the Advent of Oil." *Bulletin of Latin American Research*.

Rodríguez, Francisco, and Adam Gomolin. 2009. "Anarchy, State and Dystopia: Venezuelan Economic Institutions before the Advent of Oil." *Bulletin of Latin*

American Research 28(1): 102-21. Rodríguez, Francisco. 2007. "Cleaning up the Kitchen Sink: Growth Empirics When the World Is Not Simple." Working Paper 2006–04 (revised). Wesleyan University, Department of Economics.

Rodríguez-Clare, Andrés. 2007. "Clusters and Comparative Advantage: Implications for Industrial Policy." *Journal of Development Economics*. 82(1): 43–57.

Rodrik, D. 2006. "What's so Special about China's Exports?' Unpublished work. The Kennedy School of Government.

Romaguera, Pilar. 1991. "Wage Differentials and Efficiency Wage Models: Evidence From the Chilean Economy." Corporacion de Investigaciones Económicas para América Latina (CIEPLAN) Working Paper 153, Santiago, Chile.

Ross, Michael L. 2001. "Does Oil Hinder Democracy?" *World Politics* 53(3): 325–61.

———. "The Political Economy of the Resource Curse." *World Politics* 51(2): 297–322.

Sachs, Jeffrey D., and Andrew M. Warner. 2001a. "Fundamental Sources of Long-Run Growth." *American Economic Review, Papers and Proceedings* 87(2): 184–188.

———. 2001b. "Natural Resources and Economic Development: The Curse of Natural Resources." *European Economic Review* 45(4–6): 827–838.

———. 1999. "The Big Push, Natural Resource Booms, and Growth." *Journal of Development Economics* 59(1): 43–76.

———. 1997. "Natural Resource Abundance and Economic Growth—Revised." *Working Paper*. Harvard University, Center for International Development.

———. 1995a. "Economic Reform and the Process of Global Integration." *Brookings Papers on Economic Activity* 1: 1–95.

———. 1995b. "Natural Resource Abundance and Economic Growth." *Working Paper* 5398. Cambridge, Mass.: National Bureau of Economic Research.

Sachs, Jeffrey D., and Joaquín Vial. 2001. "Can Latin America Compete?" In The Latin American Competitiveness Report, 2001–2002, edited by Joaquín Vial and Peter K. Cornelius. Cambridge, Mass.: Center for International Development and World Economic Forum.

Sala-i-Martin, Xavier, and Arvind Subramanian. 2003. "Addressing the Resource Curse: An Illustration from Nigeria." *Working Paper* 9804. Cambridge, Mass.: National Bureau of Economic Research.

Sala-i-Martin, Xavier, Gernot Doppelhofer, and Ronald I. Miller. 2004. "Determinants of Long-Term Growth: A Bayesian Averaging of Classical Estimates (BACE) Approach." *American Economic Review* 94(4): 813–835.

Schott, Peter K. 2003. "A Comparison of Latin American and Asian Product Exports to the United States, 1972 to 1999." *Latin American Journal of Economics- formerly Cuadernos de Economía* 40(121): 414–422.

Schott, P. 2004. "Across Product versus Within Product Specialization in International Trade" *Quarterly Journal of Economics*.

Segal, Adam. 2010. "China's Innovation Wall: Beijing's Push for Homegrown Technology" *Foreign Affairs*. September 28.

Servén, Luis. 2003. "Real Exchange Rate Uncertainty and Private Investment in LDCs." *Review of Economics and Statistics* 85(1): 212–218.

Smith, Adam. 1776 [1976]. An Inquiry into the Nature and Causes of the Wealth of Nations. Oxford: Clarendon Press.

Steinfeld, Edward S. 2004. "China's Shallow Integration: Networked Production and the New Challenges for Late Industrialization" *World Development* 32(11) 1971–1987.

Stjins, Jean-Philippe. 2005. "Natural Resource Abundance and Economic Growth." *Resources Policy* 30(2): 107–130.

Summers, Robert, Alan Heston, and Bettina Aten. 2002. Penn World Table Version 6.1. University of Pennsylvania, Center for International Comparisons.

Sutton, John. 2001. *Technology and Market Structure*. MIT Press: Cambridge, MA.

Tornell, Aaron, and Philip R. Lane. 1999. "The Voracity Effect." *American Economic Review* 89(1): 22–46.

Trefler, Daniel. 1995. "The Case of the Missing Trade and Other Mysteries." *American Economic Review* 85(5): 1029–1046.

Tyson. Laura D'Andrea. 1992. *Who's Bashing Whom: Trade Conflict in High Technology Industries*. Institute for International Economics: Washington, DC.

UNESCO. 1980. *Statistical Yearbook*. United Nations, Paris.

van der Ploeg, Frederick. 2011. "Natural Resources: Curse or Blessing?" *Journal of Economic Literature*, 49(2): 366–420.

Verhoogen, E. 2008. "Trade, Quality Upgrading, and Wage Inequality in the Mexican Manufacturing Sector." *Quarterly Journal of Economics* 123(2): 489–530.

Vettas, Nikolaos. 2000. "Investment dynamics in markets with endogenous demand." *The Journal of Industrial Economics*. 48(2): 189–203.

Viner, Jacob. 1952. International Trade and Economic Development. Glencoe, Ill: Free Press.

Vollrath, T.L. 1991. "A Theoretical Evaluation of Alternative Trade Intensity Measures of Revealed Comparative Advantage." *Review of World Economics/ Welwirtschaftliches Archiv* 130: 265–279.

Wacziarg, Romain, and Karen Horn Welch. 2002. "Integration and Growth: An Update." Stanford University.

Watkins, Melville. 1963. "A Staple Theory of Economic Growth." *Canadian Journal of Economics and Political Science* 29(2): 141–158.

Waugh, Michael. 2008. "Human Capital, Product Quality, and Bilateral Trade. Unpublished Work." Federal Reserve Bank of Minneapolis, Minnesota.

Wei, S.J. 1999. "Currency Hedging and Goods Trade." *European Economic Review* 43 (7): 1371–1394.

Wright, Gavin, and Jesse W. Czelusta. 2007. "Resource-Based Growth Past and Present." In Natural Resources: Neither Curse nor Destiny, edited by Daniel Lederman and William F. Maloney, chapter 7. Stanford University Press.

Wright, Gavin. 2001. "Resource Based Growth, Then and Now." Stanford University.

Young, Alwyn. 2002. "A Tale of Two Cities" in NBER Macro Economics Annual 1992, MIT Press, Cambridge.

Index

Boeing, 3
Bolivia
  PRODY goods in, 30
  wage premiums in, 38*b*
Brambilla, Irene, 35–36, 37*b*, 40,
    42, 46, 48, 53
Bravo-Ortega, Claudio, 20
Brazil
  aircraft industry in, 81
  EXPYs in, 27
  human capital in, 83
  natural resources in, 22*n*3
  patents in, 78, 79*f*
  wage premiums in, 36, 38*b*
Breznitz, Dan, 86
Broda, C., 100
Brooks, E., 76*n*1

C

Caballero, R. J., 100
Cadot, Olivier, 104*n*1
Canada
  economic diversification in, 21
  natural resources in, 14
Caribbean countries. *See also*
    specific countries
  education in, 40, 41*t*
  export quality levels in, 59,
    62*b*, 75
  export unit values in, 59–66,
    60–61*f*, 62*b*, 63–65*f*,
    68, 75
  incumbent goods in, 73, 74*f*
  mobility costs in, 36
  revealed comparative
    advantage in, 81, 89*n*2
  skill premiums in, 42, 47*t*,
    48, 53
  volatility indicators for, 95,
    96*t*, 97
  wage premiums in, 35
Carrere, Celine, 104*n*1
Central Asia, incumbent goods
    in, 73, 74*f*
Chaudhuri, Shubham, 36
Chile

clothing exports in, 66
copper exports in, 77–78, 82
diversification of goods in, 32
education in, 38
entry and exit patterns in, 74
EXPYs in, 28
footwear exports in, 66
high-tech industries in, 88
human capital in, 83
skilled workers in, 40
wage premiums and, 36, 38*b*
wine exports in, 61
China, People's Republic of
  economic growth in, 16
  electronic manufacturing
    goods in, 8, 84, 85–86,
    85*b*
  export quality levels in, 62*b*
  EXPYs in, 27
  externalities and, 2
  high productivity goods in, 26
  production chains and, 86,
    88–89
  value added goods in, 86, 88*t*
Clark, P., 100
clothing exports, 66
CODELCO (National
    Copper Corporation
    of Chile), 77
coffee, 60–61
Colombia
  clothing exports in, 66
  education in, 38
  EXPYs in, 28
  footwear exports in, 66
  skilled workers in, 40
  wage premiums in, 36, 38*b*
commodities
  "commodity currencies," 101
  "commodity manufactures,"
    85
  dependence on, 95
  natural hedge for, 100–102
  quality ladder and, 7, 60, 75
comparative advantage. *See*
    revealed comparative
    advantage